CSS for Beginners

Learn to Tweak Your Website Design

Dr. Andy Williams

http://ezseonews.com

Version 1.6.
Published 17th September 2013

Contents

LEGAL STUFF

Recommended CSS Editors

CSS is an abbreviation for Cascading Style Sheets. Put simply, it's a style sheet language that web designers use for easily modifying the look format, and layout, of a web page. You can edit CSS in any text editor (such as Microsoft Windows Notepad), or your preferred HTML editor. However, there are some excellent commercial tools available that really help with CSS. The real value of a dedicated CSS editor is in making sure your CSS syntax is correct. With an editor, you don't need to remember the syntax for each bit of code your write because the tool does it for you. This means you're free to work on your design without having to worry about CSS coding.

I use a great tool called **TopStyle** which you can get from here:

http://svanas.dynip.com/TopStyle/

You can download a trial version of TopStyle, but it does have some serious limitations. If you don't want to pay too much for a CSS editor, but would still like a dedicated program to help you with your CSS, then a cheaper alternative is a program called **Rapid CSS**, which is still pretty good. You can get that from here:

http://www.blumentals.net/rapidcss/

Both of these tools save you time and will make your job easier, but they are PC only software. If you are a Mac user, Style Master is a good alternative. You can get that from here:

http://www.westciv.com/style_master/

Macrabbit used to have a really good CSS tool called CSS Edit. That doesn't seem to be available as a standalone CSS editor anymore, but it is integrated into their Expresso web editor software. You can download a 15-day trial of Expresso from here:

http://macrabbit.com/espresso/

In this book, I'll be using and showing screenshots from TopStyle, but if you are using another tool, or text editor, then don't worry. The editor is there just to make sure the syntax is correct, and you can follow along with any editor of your choice.

How & Why You Should Use the TopStyle Demo as You Work Through This Book

There is a very good reason why you should use CSS software, rather than a text editor while learning CSS, and that's because you don't need to remember any syntax. Since I am using TopStyle in this book, I recommend you download the trial version and follow along.

It's easy to migrate to a different CSS editor (or just use a text editor), once you understand the "language" of CSS.

How to Use This Book

In order to be able to tweak and modify your own website template, whether that's a WordPress blog, HTML site, or other, you do need to understand some CSS basics.

The main part of this book will give you a comprehensive understanding of CSS, and by the time you've read through to the end, you can start looking at the CSS behind some real websites, and furthermore, you'll be able to look through that code with confidence.

All source code in this tutorial can be downloaded from the link found in the Appendix at the end of the book. I encourage you to do this so that you can look at the examples in a full size browser.

If you want to view any of the source code, you can open all of the files in a text editor (or a CSS editor of your choice). If you want to see what the web page looks like, simply open the HTML file in your web browser.

At the end of this book there is a link to videos that I have created. These show you how to apply your newly acquired CSS knowledge to problem-solve, investigate, and tweak your web page design to exactly how you want it to appear.

1. Introduction

Simply put, CSS (Cascading Style Sheets) is a very powerful "mechanism" that webmasters use to help them design, and then further maintain, the look and feel of their sites with a minimum amount of effort.

In this chapter, I want to whet your appetite for style sheets and show you their real potential on how simple it can be to change fonts, colors, spacing etc., of a Web document. In the remainder of this book, I'll show you how to do this by yourself.

I am going to show you some examples and provide the source code of those pages with screenshots. Whenever screenshots are of source code, you will see a filename after them in brackets, e.g., (1.1.html). In the Appendix at the back of this book, there is a link where you can download all of the source code from these pages. The filename after the screenshot tells you the name of the file in that download.

OK, let's begin with a very simple example.

You probably know about those awfully large H1 header tags that are often set as the default. To make your site look more professional, you might want to reduce the size of these headers. You could just use an H2 or H3 header instead, but then you risk losing the possible SEO benefits of an H1 tag. It is always better to use the correct headers for the correct task. H1 headers should always go at the top of the page and are used as the opening headline.

Using CSS, you can make them tinier, but then you can also make them smaller using standard HTML tags, so why bother with CSS you might be thinking?

Have a look at the source code of the page below. It uses HTML tags in to control the sizes of the font:

```
4   <html>
5   <head>
6   <meta http-equiv="Content-Type" content="text/html;
    charset=iso-8859-1">
7   <title>H1 Header made smaller</title>
8   </head>
9
10  <body>
11  <h1><font size="2">This is an H1 header </font></h1>
12  <p><font size="+5">And this is regular text made
    bigger. </font></p>
13  </body>
14  </html>
15
```

(1.1.html)

This is what that web page actually looks like:

This is an H1 header

And this is regular text made bigger.

See how I have made the regular text much larger than the H1 header?

I can even control the fonts using HTML tags in the document.

5

Here, take a look at the source code of this page:

```html
<body>
<h1><font size="2" face="Verdana, Arial, Helvetica,
sans-serif">This is an H1 header </font></h1>
<p><font size="+5" face="Verdana, Arial, Helvetica,
sans-serif">And this is regular text made bigger.
</font></p>
</body>
</html>
```

(1.2.html)

This page looks like this:

This is an H1 header

And this is regular text made bigger.

Notice how the font is now different from the first example.

Now look at this page. Here it uses CSS to control the size and the font style of the text:

This is an H1 header

And this is regular text made bigger.

It looks identical to the last example, and it is. But, this one uses CSS to modify the font size and fonts style of the text.

Here is the HTML code of the webpage:

```html
<html>
<head>
<meta http-equiv="Content-Type" content="text/html;
charset=iso-8859-1">
<title>H1 Header made smaller</title>
<link rel="stylesheet" href="1.3.css"
type="text/css">
</head>

<body>
<h1>This is an H1 header</h1>
<p>And this is regular text made bigger.</p>
</body>
</html>
```

(1.3.html & 1.3.css)

Notice that the code specifies the H1 header, and how the normal text looks regular. There are no specific instructions there to change the size of the fonts. You'll also notice that there is a new line in this webpage that specifies a **style.css** file.

The syle.css file gives web browser instructions on how to style the header and the normal text. So let's take a look at what's inside this file.

```
h1 {
      font-size: smaller;
      font-family: Verdana, Geneva, Arial,
      Helvetica, sans-serif;
}


p {

      font-family: Verdana, Geneva, Arial,
      Helvetica, sans-serif;
      font-size: 6ex;
}
```

(1.3.css)

The file specifies formatting instructions for the h1 header tag and also text inside the <p> tags, with <p> representing paragraphs.

Do you see how there is no HTML formatting tags in the source code of the page using CSS? All the page does is specifying which text is an H1 header, and which text is a paragraph. And do you also see that the non-CSS pages need to have the HTML tags to tell the web browser which fonts and sizes to use?

The size of the non-CSS webpage is larger than the one using a CSS "style sheet", and it's far more complex. Imagine a much longer webpage and how bloated it would become if all formatting commands were embedded inside the html document.

So, one of the main benefits of using a style sheet to control the formatting for your site, is that it reduces the size of the web pages. Your web browser will download the style sheet ONCE, and then apply it to every page site-wide.

Imagine you have 100 pages on a site and you want to change the font sizes and colors on all 100 pages. If you have used HTML to specify size and style of your fonts, you will then need to manually go in and change 100 pages. However, if you use CSS to control the size and style, you only need to edit one file, and that is your CSS style sheet.

To demonstrate, look at this web page:

> This is an H1 header
>
> # And this is regular text made bigger.

(1.4.html and 1.4.css)

The source of that web page is identical to the source of this one:

> **This is an H1 header**
>
> ## And this is regular text made bigger.

(1.5.html and 1.5.css)

The only difference between these two pages is the style sheet I have used for each one.

The first page:

```css
h1 {
    font-size: larger;
    font-family: "Courier New", Courier,
    monospace;
    background: Yellow;
    border: thin dashed #66CE00;
    font-weight: lighter;
    line-height: 50px;
    text-align: center;
}

p {
    font-family: "Courier New", Courier,
    monospace;
    font-size: 12ex;
    font: small-caps;
    color: Green;
}
```

(1.4.css)

The second page:

```css
h1 {
    font-size: smaller;
    font-family: Verdana, Geneva, Arial,
    Helvetica, sans-serif;
}

p {
    font-family: Verdana, Geneva, Arial,
    Helvetica, sans-serif;
    font-size: 6ex;
}
```

(1.5.css)

This means that by editing just one file - the style sheet - I was able to make sweeping changes to the appearance of not only that page, but every other page using that same style sheet.

On a 100 page site, using CSS to control the appearance means that all 100 pages would have changed the moment I uploaded my edited style sheet. Now can you see the potential?

Have a look at the source code of these two HTML documents:

Example Web Page #1

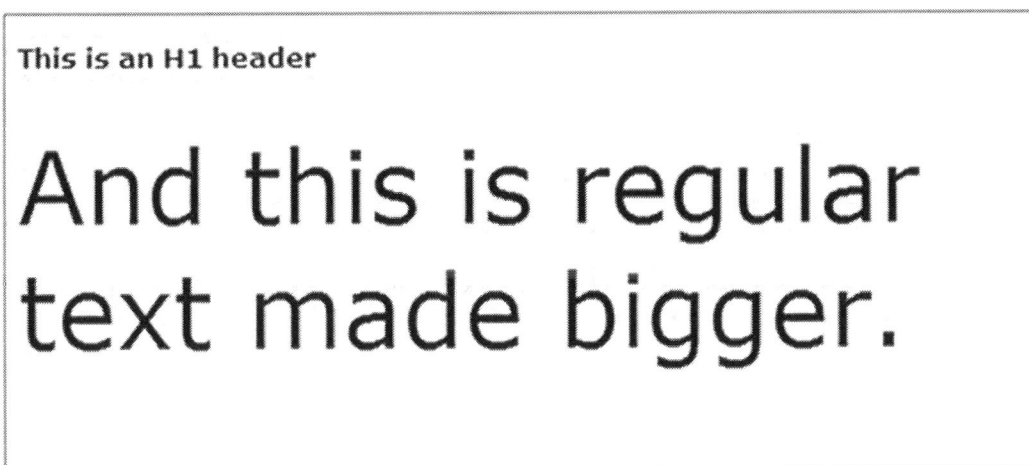

This is an H1 header

And this is regular text made bigger.

(1.6.hmtl)

Example Web Page #2

```
This is an H1 header
```

And this is regular text made bigger.

(1.7.html and 1.7.css)

Which would you imagine was the bigger file (and remember bigger files mean slower loading).

Well, the second page looks more complicated, but here are the file sizes:

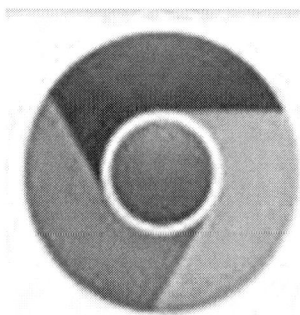

1.6.html

Chrome HTML Document

Date modified: 22/11/2012 16:20

Size: 487 bytes

1.7.html

Chrome HTML Document

Date modified: 27/11/2012 09:58

Size: 406 bytes

The second page uses CSS to create a smaller file size.

The formatting of a web page that uses CSS has all of its style commands in the CSS file, not in the HTML document, thus making the HTML file is smaller:

```
h1 {
        font-size: larger;
        font-family: "Courier New", Courier,
        monospace;
        background: Yellow;
        border: thin dashed #66CE00;
        font-weight: lighter;
        line-height: 50px;
        text-align: center;
}

p {
        font-family: "Courier New", Courier,
        monospace;
        font-size: 12ex;
        font: small-caps;
        color: Green;
        }
```

(1.7.css)

Now you may be thinking that it's not that much smaller, but we are talking about a page here that has very little content.

IMPORTANT

If you have given any thought to the space savings, then you've probably wondered about the size of the style sheet. E.g., if my style sheet was 2 Kb in size, and the web page was say 10Kb, surely that means the browser needs to download a total of 12 Kb for the page - right?

Well, yes, and no, is the answer to that, so let me explain. You see, the browser will cache the style sheet, meaning that it will be downloaded only once, and then remembered and applied to all the pages that use it. So once the style sheet has been downloaded for the first time, the browser will only need to download the HTML files from that point on.

Let's look at the math involved.

A few years ago I converted a site from inline formatting to using an external CSS file (as we have seen in the examples so far). The site had a total of 106 pages. The homepage went from 45Kb down to 18Kb, and the style sheet for the site was 28 Kb.

If we assume that all pages on the site were roughly the same size in Kb, then the total download size of the site before the conversion would have been:

45 x 106 = 4,770 Kb

After conversion, the download size of the site was:

(18 x 106) + 28 = 1,936 Kb

(106 times the average file size plus the CSS file ONCE).

That's almost 60% smaller for the site as a whole, simply by using a style sheet as the method of formatting.

What I have shown you so far is only the beginning. CSS can be used to position elements on your page, such as placing menus on the right or the left, for example. While it's quite possible to create layouts with HTML tables, using CSS means quicker loading times for the pages, and smaller, less-complex code, which improves crawl-ability for search engines.

In this CSS tutorial, I am going to show you how to do all of this for yourself!

2. Table-less Page Layouts

In the last chapter I gave you an introduction to Cascading Style Sheets (CSS) by showing you some examples of text formatting using CSS. You also saw how quickly you could change the look and feel of a complete site, by changing one file - the style sheet.

Now we'll continue on with this introduction by looking at another powerful use of CSS, which is the table-less web page layout. I will show you some simple examples of what is possible.

Remember, this chapter is just an overview. I won't be showing you how to do it for yourself - just yet. This is something we will cover later in the book, so for now, just sit back and relax.

Let's start off by looking at a web page that has been laid out using tables. Look at this page, and examine the source code:

Page Header		
Left Menu Main Page Text		Right Menu
Page Footer		

(2.1.html)

Those of you familiar with HTML tables will see a simple three-column, three-row table. Some of the cells have been joined to form the header and footer. This simple file is 749 bytes in size.

Here is the HTML:

```
<body>
<table width="100%" border="1" cellpadding="2" cellspacing="2"
 bordercolor="#FFFFFF">
<tr bordercolor="#0000FF">
 <td colspan="3"><div align="center">Page Header </div></td>
</tr>
<tr>
 <td width="17%" bordercolor="#0000FF">Left Menu </td>
 <td width="63%">Main Page Text</td>
 <td width="20%" bordercolor="#0000FF">Right Menu </td>
</tr>
<tr bordercolor="#0000FF">
 <td colspan="3"><div align="center">Page Footer </div></td>
</tr>
</table>
</body>
```

OK, now let's look at another page that has a similar layout, only this one uses CSS instead:

Page Header		
Left Menu	Main Page	Right Menu
Page Footer		

(2.2.html and 2.2.css)

The style sheet for this layout has separate sections for the header, footer, left and right sidebars, and the main content column.

Here is the CSS code for the 'page header' section, taken from the style sheet:

```
div#header {
    position: absolute;
    left: -1px;
    top: 8px;
    width:100%;
    height:90px;
    z-index: 1
    border-top-color: Blue;
    border-top-style: solid;
    border-top-width: 1px;
    border-bottom-color: Blue;
    border-bottom-style: solid;
    border-bottom-width: 1px;
    border-left-color: Blue;
    border-left-style: solid;
    border-left-width: 1px;
    border-right-color: Blue;
    border-right-style: solid;
    border-right-width: 1px;
    }
```

I won't show you the entire style sheet here. If you are interested in seeing the whole thing, check out the file "2.2.css" in the source code (see the Appendix).

This table-less layout is smaller than the HTML document, which uses tables to create its page layout. Here is the body section of the table-less layout:

```
11  <div id="main">
12     <p>Main Page <br>
13     </p>
14  </div>
15
16  <div id="left">  Left Menu</div>
17
18  <div id="right">Right Menu </div>
19
20  <div id="header">
21     <div align="center">Page Header </div>
22  </div>
23
24  <div id="footer">
25     <div align="center">Page Footer </div>
26  </div>
27
```

(2.2.html)

You will notice that there are no table tags at all. Each section of the page (main content, header, sidebars, and footer sections), is contained in its own little block of code. And each of these blocks of code starts with a line that tells the web browser how to format that particular section.

Note: Don't worry if it all seems a little confusing. I can promise that if you just keep reading, it will all start to come together before you know it.

<div id="main"> YOUR MAIN CONTENT GOES HERE </div>

This code defines a block of code that the web browser should format using the "**main**" ID which can be found in the style sheet.

Note: This WILL all start to make a lot more sense as you go through the tutorial. So don't become disheartened if you are finding things a little difficult to grasp right now. I can promise that if you just keep reading, it will all start to come together before you know it.

OK, so if we compare the table, and table-less html files, there isn't that much difference in the size of the two pages. However, the look of the CSS one is both crisper and clearer to the eye.

The positioning of the page layout using CSS is done with pinpoint accuracy, whereas the page designed with tables is more likely to suffer problems as you add more content. You will probably need to use graphics to help space out the horizontal and vertical columns too, something in itself that only adds to the workload.

OK, now look at this page:

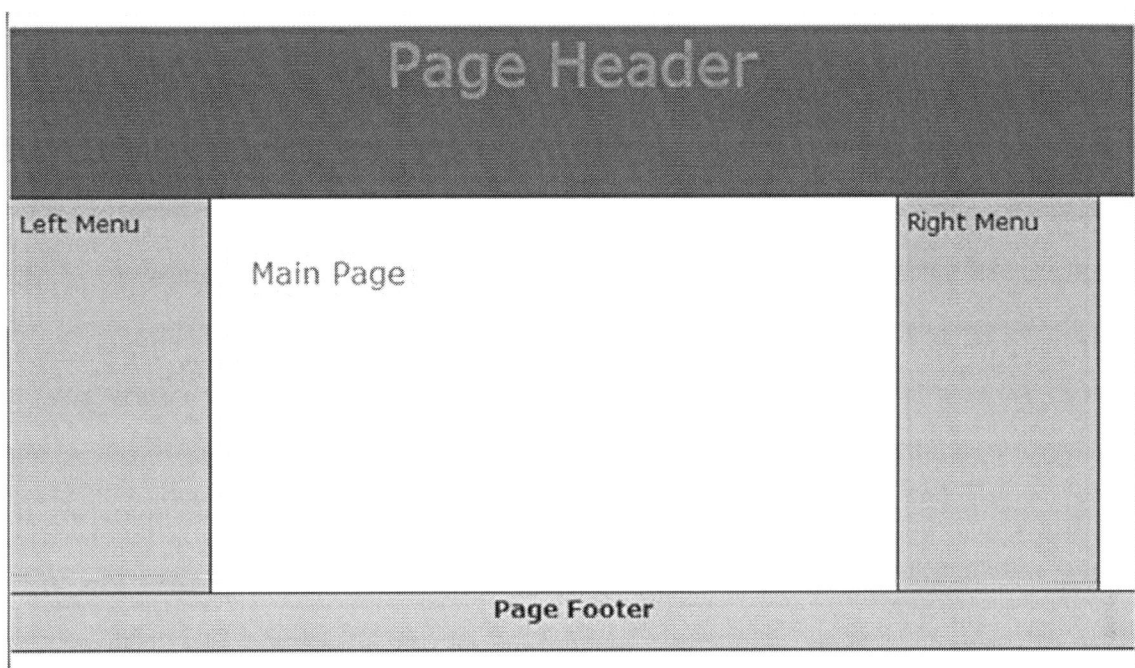

(2.3.html & 2.3.css)

The HTML code behind the page is IDENTICAL to the HTML of 2.2.html:

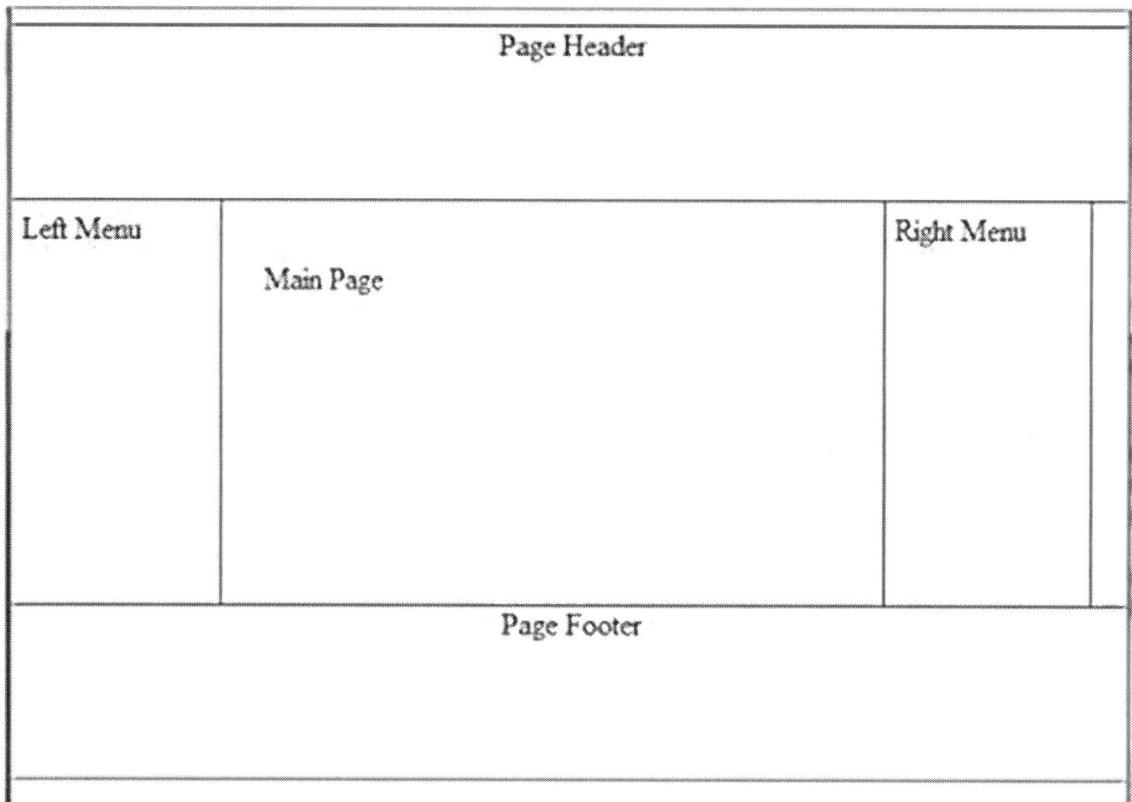

Page Header		
Left Menu	Main Page	Right Menu
Page Footer		

The only difference here is that I have edited the style sheet.

Now compare 2.2.css & 2.3.css

Imagine if you had 100 pages on your site, and all you had to do in order to dramatically change the entire look of every page was to modify just ONE file. Are you seeing the potential of CSS?

How big would a template like this be if it were built using tables?

Let's see. Here is my design using tables:

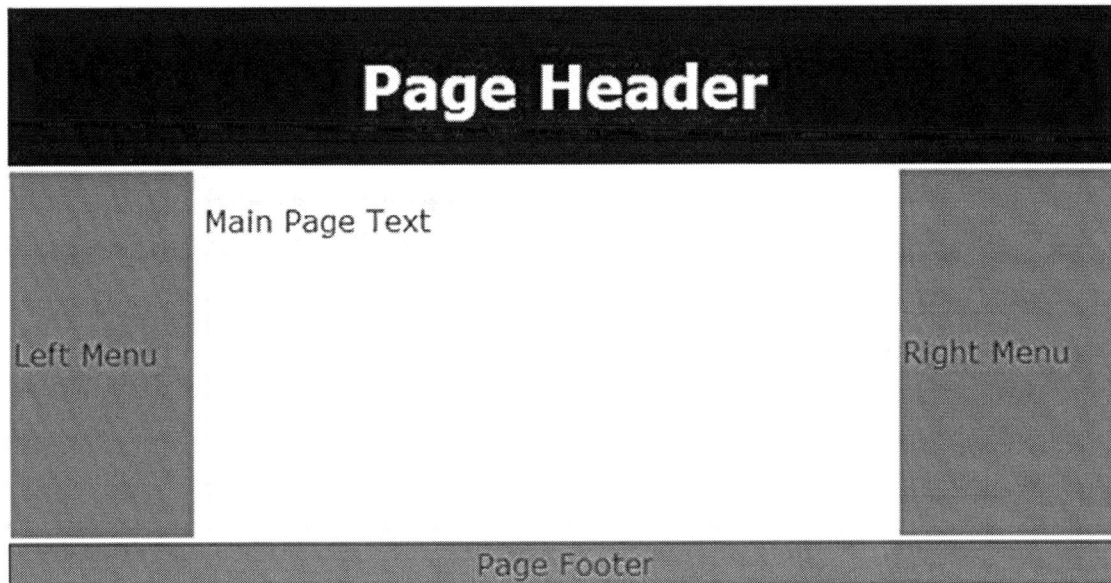

(2.4.html)

The table layout is 1.16 Kb

2.4.html
Chrome HTML Document
Date modified: 22/11/2012 16:20
Size: 1.16 KB

The equivalent CSS layout is just 590 bytes (1,024 bytes = 1 kb).

2.3.html
Chrome HTML Document
Date modified: 27/11/2012 10:06
Size: 590 bytes

That's about 50% of the table layout size.

Summary

In the first two chapter of this book, I hope I have shown you the tremendous potential for using CSS in website construction and maintenance.

As for the remainder of this book, I will be showing you how to understand, edit, and use CSS for yourself. We will start at the very beginning and go through the process in baby steps. My goal is not only to make you confident using CSS, but to become good at it too.

3. CSS Basics

So far, I've shown you some simple examples of what CSS can do. It's now time for you to learn how to use it for yourself. I will guide you through this one step at a time, ensuring that this tutorial is easy to follow. If you don't understand one section, then my advice is to take a short break, and then come back and re-read it.

Note: You do need a basic knowledge of HTML.

What you have observed so far is how easily you can change the look of your website using CSS. This includes changing text attributes like the color, and size, etc., but also the page layout. We've seen how modifying a single style sheet can make sweeping changes to an entire website.

For CSS to work effectively, the webpage needs to communicate with the style sheet. The web browser will need to be able to identify the formatting for say an H1 header, so that it can render that header on the visible webpage.

The style sheet needs specific rules that tell the browser, for example, to make the H1 headers blue. In return, the web page needs instructions to tell the browser to look in the style sheet for H1 formatting. We'll simply call these instructions "rules".

Let's look at the structure of a simple rule.

In the style sheet, each rule begins with a "Selector". This defines which HTML tag you want the rule applied to. We then get some curly brackets to hold the properties of the rule.

Here is a simple rule:

```
h1 {
   color: blue
}
```

This can also be written on a single line, like this:

```
h1 { color: blue }
```

Note that white space does not affect the rule. Usually, when building a CSS style sheet, we tend to spread rules out onto separate lines. This is just to make them easier to read and modify.

This particular rule starts off by the selector "h1". In this case, it will tell the browser to make all H1 headers blue.

Here is another rule with a bit more instruction:

H2 {
color:red;
font-family:Arial, Verdana, serif;
font-size:18px;
}

Again, this could be written like this:

H2 { color:red; font-family: Arial, Verdana, serif; font-size:18px; }

This rule will make all H2 tags red, size 18px, and use the font family "arial, verdana, serif".

I have only added a few properties to this rule, but there are many more I could use. Now, if you are a complete beginner to all of this, I know what you are thinking. With so many properties, how on earth am I going to remember them all?

Well, that is one of the main reasons I use TopStyle CSS & HTML Editor. If you use TopStyle, or Rapid CSS (or any other dedicated CSS editor), then you don't need to remember the properties. The software will prompt you with the full suite of properties for any particular tag.

Here is a screenshot of TopStyle 5.0. Don't worry if you can't see the details; it's only the layout I want you to observe here.

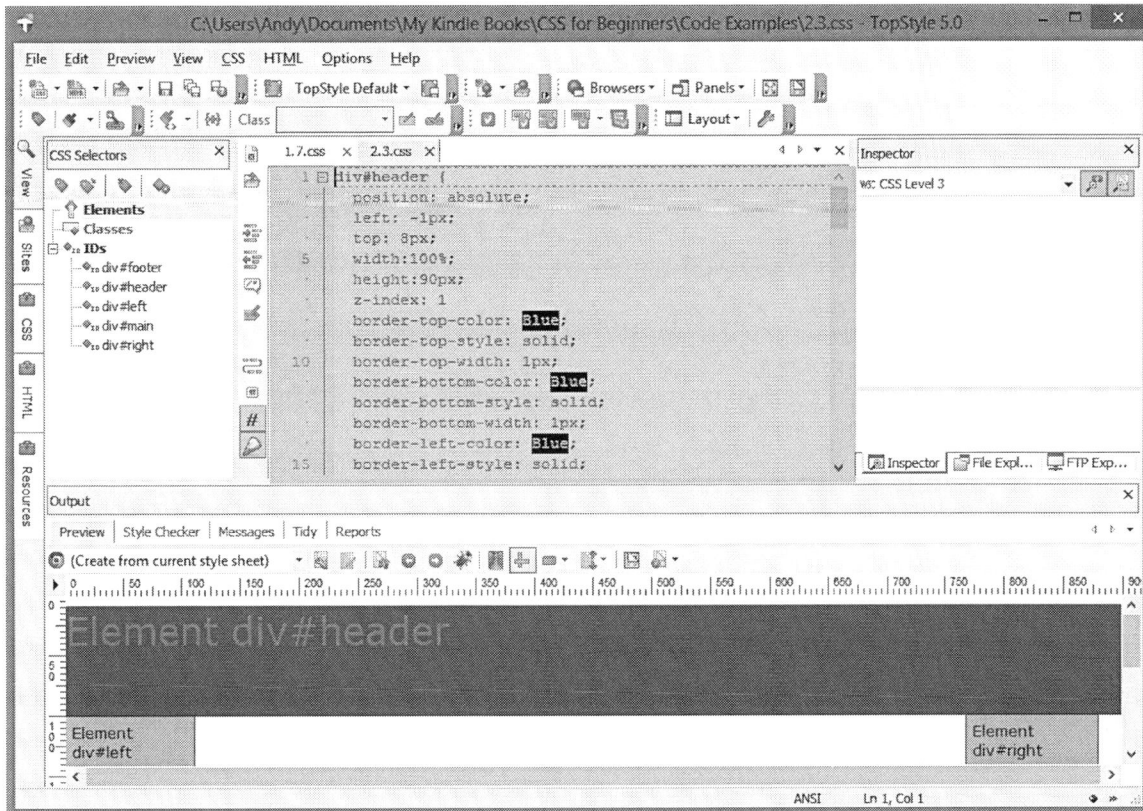

I've highlighted the CSS code from one of our examples in the book.

The bottom part of the Editor is a preview of the styles defined in that style sheet. So we can now see the familiar CSS layout with header, left and right sidebars, main content area, and the footer (which is just out of the screenshot).

NOTE: You can download and install the free version of TopStyle. As I mentioned earlier, it does have a lot of limitations, but it's still a great tool for helping you as you learn CSS.

Another alternative CSS Editor is Rapid CSS. This one is cheaper than TopStyle, but still quite powerful:

I can highly recommend both TopStyle Pro and Rapid CSS. Go and look at both sites for their current prices and features, and you can rest assured whichever one you buy, you will end up with a quality product.

OK, before we continue any further with this, there is one more thing you need to know so that you can start to play around with CSS, and that is where do you put the rules that you create?

We have already talked about the style sheet, which is the file that holds all of the CSS rules. The style sheet will be uploaded to your website server along with all the web pages.

Note: If you are using WordPress, the style sheet is a separate file found in the WordPress template folder:

In this screenshot you can see my WordPress theme in the top Window. It's called Lifestyle. In the lower window, you can see the files inside the template folder, including the style.css file. This file holds ALL of the formatting information for my entire site.

So you might be wondering how the web page knows where to look for the formatting rules - right? Well, you just need to add the line of code below into your web page (WordPress users don't have to worry as WordPress will add the line for you).

<link rel="style sheet" media="screen" type="text/css" href="styles.css">

NOTE: In this example, the style sheet is called "styles.css".

In 'Code View', place this single line of code just before the </head> tag of the web page.

```
<html>
<head>
<title></title>

<link rel="style sheet" media="screen" type="text/css"
href="styles.css">

</head>
```

Things to Try Yourself

OK, I think we have covered enough for this section, but I'd like to finish with something you can try for yourself.

1. Create a simple web page that has an H1 header on it.
2. Add the line of code mentioned above so that it will use a style sheet.
3. Create a text file and save it with the name: styles.css
4. Add an h1 rule to the styles.css file and make the H1 headers "blue".

Once done, upload the web page and the CSS file to your server, and then open it in your browser. Does your h1 header appear blue? It should do!

Now, modify the styles.css file to make the h1 header red, size 18, and font family "Arial, Verdana, serif". Save and upload the CSS file overwriting the current one.

OK, so now go back to the web page again (or click refresh in your browser if you still have it open). Has your H1 header changed? It should have done if you followed the code rules.

Now, imagine you have a 100 page website, each linking to the styles.css file. What if you wanted to change the look of all H1 headers on your site? With CSS, it means you only have to edit one bit of code in a single file, and then every H1 spread over 100 webpages would have changed the second you saved and uploaded the modified styles.css file. Are you getting excited yet?

In the next section, we will look at the most important selectors you can use to modify the look of your webpage, and you'll also get the chance to try out more tweaking for yourself. I'll be using TopStyle, but you can use a text editor, Rapid CSS, Dreamweaver, or any web editor you have at your disposal.

4. Using TopStyle for Editing Style Sheets

In this chapter, we are going to look at how to use TopStyle to create and modify style sheets. If you are using a text-based editor, just follow along and manually type in the selectors and properties.

OK, start TopStyle.

We have seen some "selectors" in previous parts of this book, like h1 and h2, so let us now see how we can use TopStyle to create a style sheet that will modify our h1 tags for us.

Start by creating a new file, and save it somewhere on your hard disk.

Now move your mouse over the toolbar of TopStyle and find the button that creates a "new selector". It's over on the left there, in the **CSS Selectors** section:

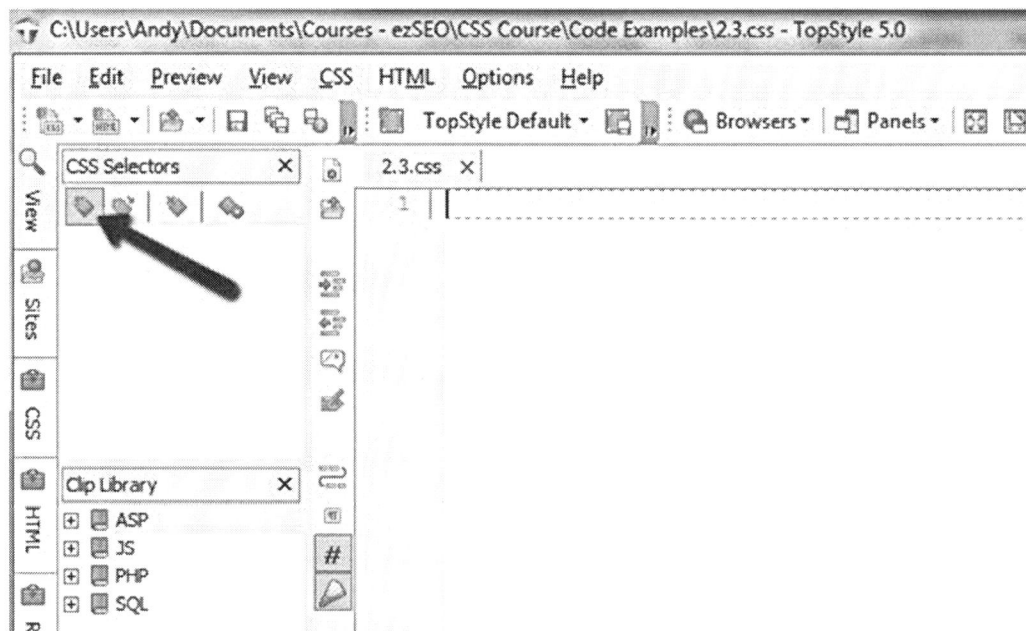

Click the button, and a window appears.

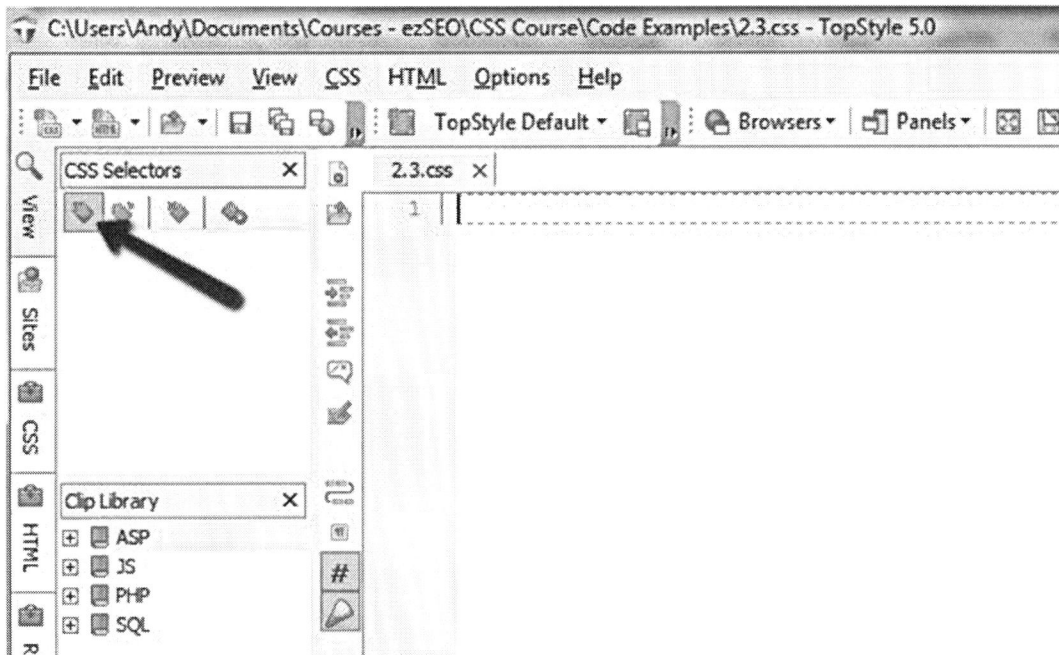

Along the top of this screen are a few tabs. Click on the one named **Simple**.

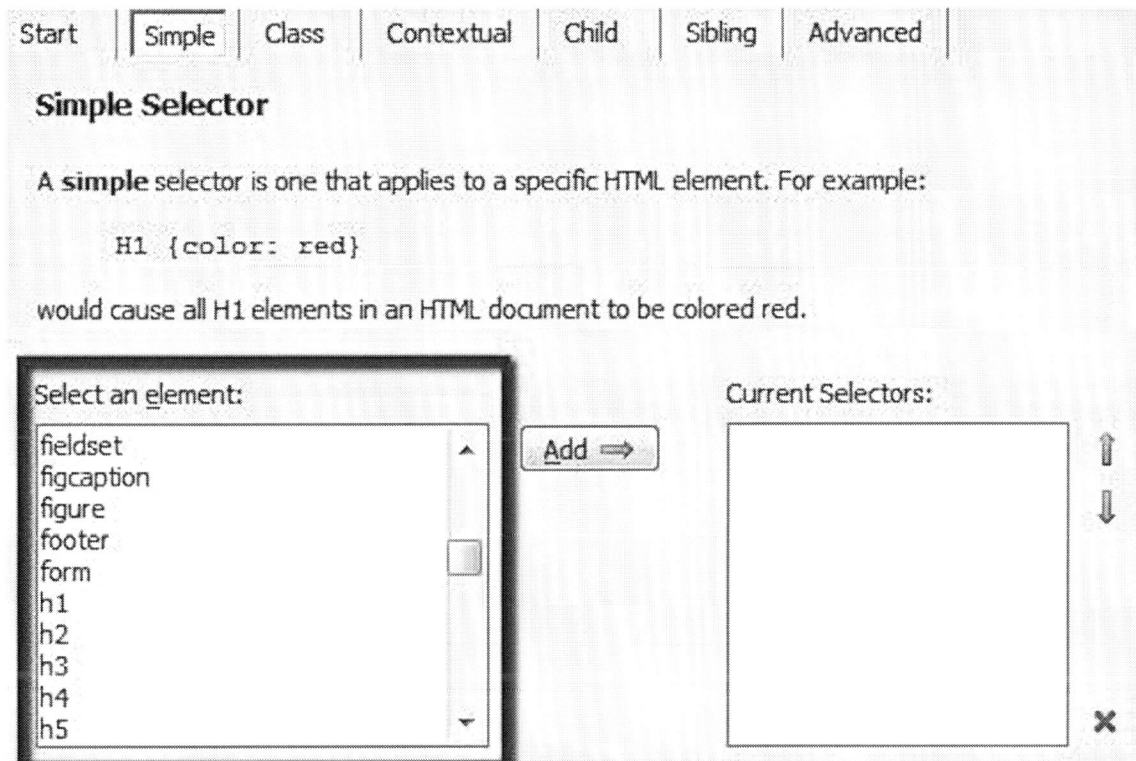

On the left, you will see a scroll box that holds all of the HTML elements that you can use for creating your rules. Let's select the h1 header and modify it.

Click h1 in the list:

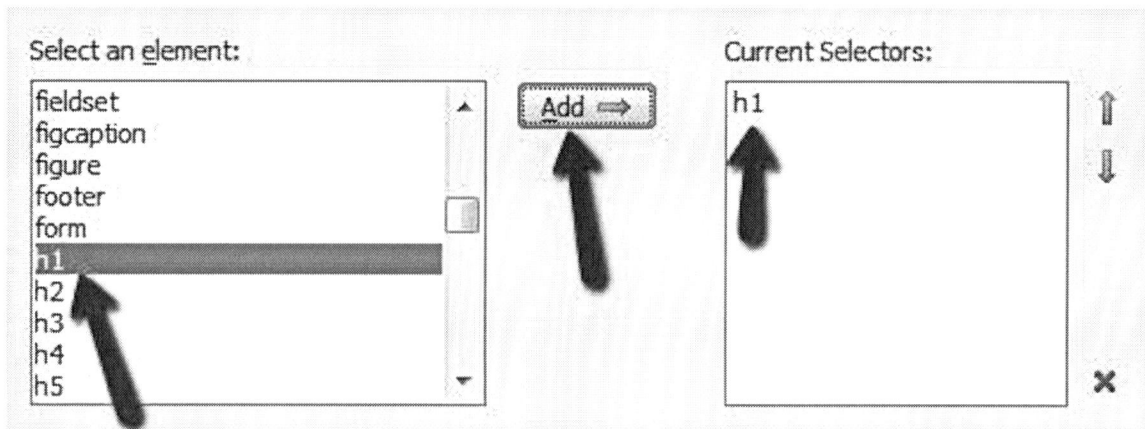

Once the h1 is highlighted, click the "Add" button. You should now see h1 appear in the "Current Selector" box on the right, indicating that this is the element we want to modify.

Now click the "OK" button to create this rule.

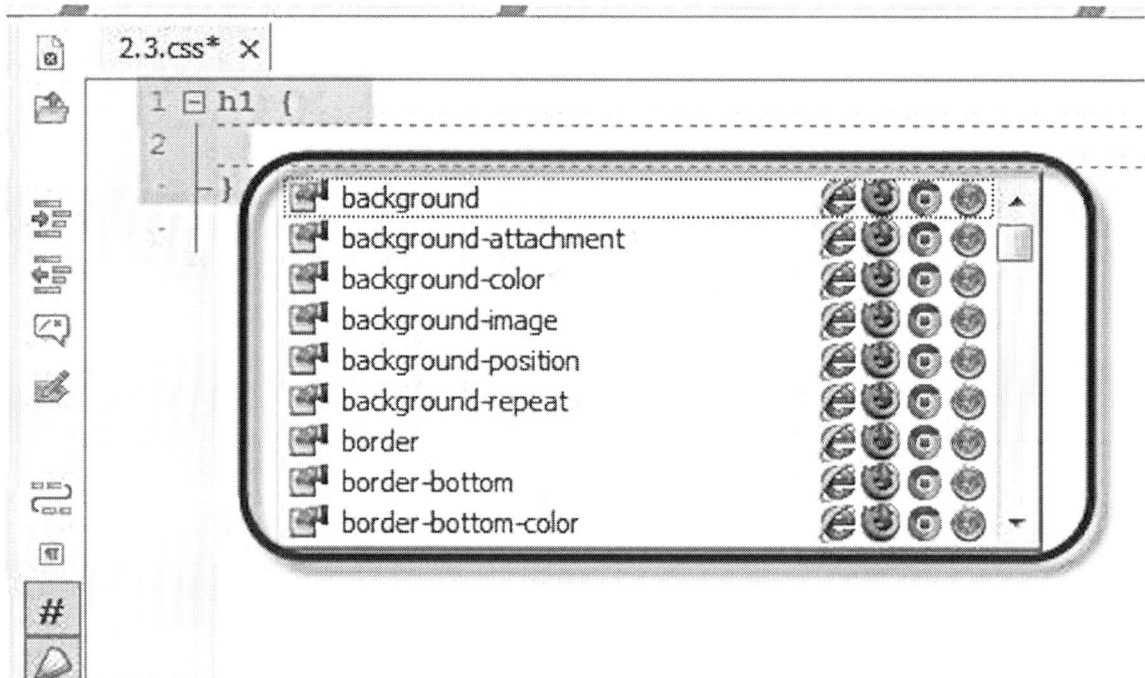

In the main CSS window, you will see the rule has been created with the selector and a pair of empty curly brackets. There are no properties yet, but TopStyle presents us with a list of them to add as we like.

If you remember, the curly brackets are there to hold the parameters for the selector. Your cursor will be flashing inside the curly brackets.

OK, let's start by modifying the color of our h1 tags.

On the right of the screen is the "**Style Inspector**".

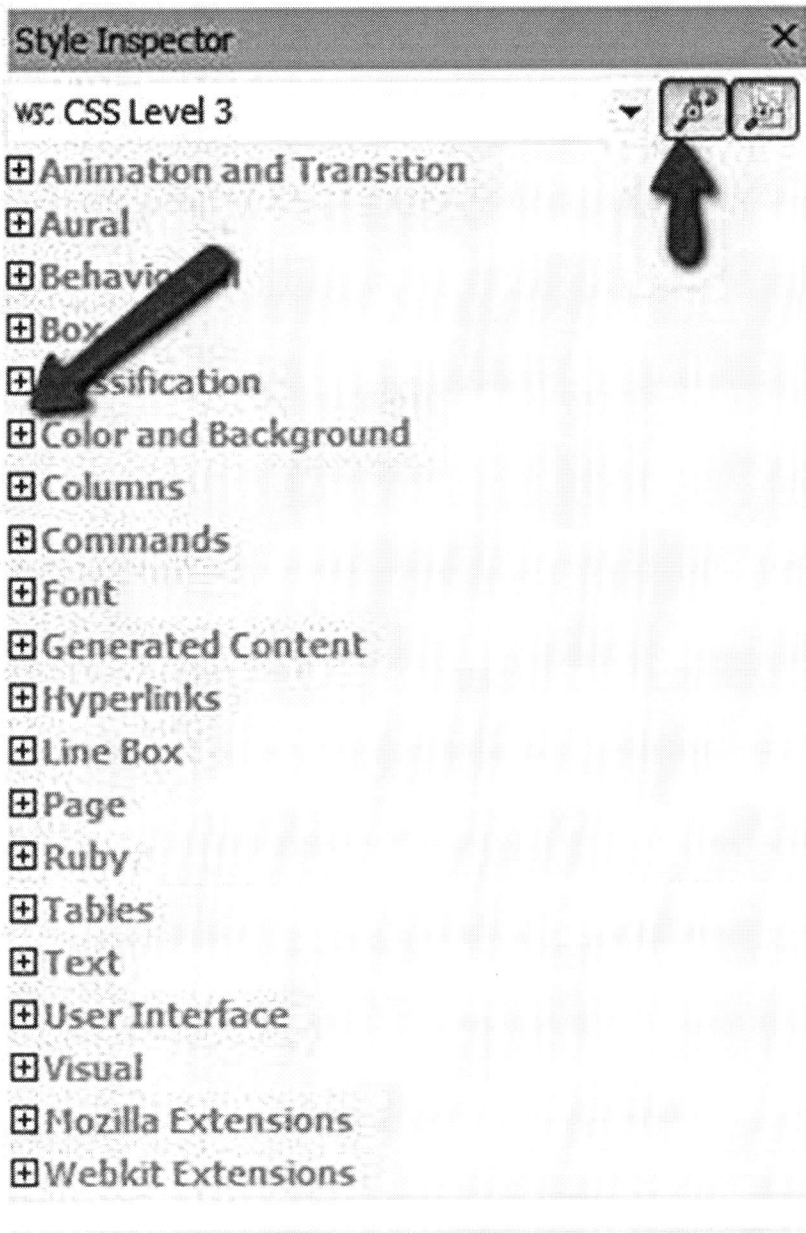

On the top right of this screen is a button that "categorizes" the properties. Click it 'On' and 'Off' and watch the contents of the Style Inspector change. When you've had your fun, make sure the button is clicked in the "down" position.

You'll notice that at the top of the Style Inspector it says **CSS Level 3**. As with anything, CSS has evolved, with new properties being added over time. CSS Level 3 is the current incarnation at the time of writing this book. As such, it has far more properties than earlier versions of CSS. For this tutorial though, we do not need to clutter up the Inspector with all of these categories and properties, because it will only make it difficult to find anything. As you become more experienced with CSS, you can change this back to CSS Level 3 if you want to.

So for now, I suggest you change this to CSS Level 1. This will have most of the CSS properties that we will cover in this book (we will change to Level 2 or higher later though, for a property that isn't Level 1 compatible).

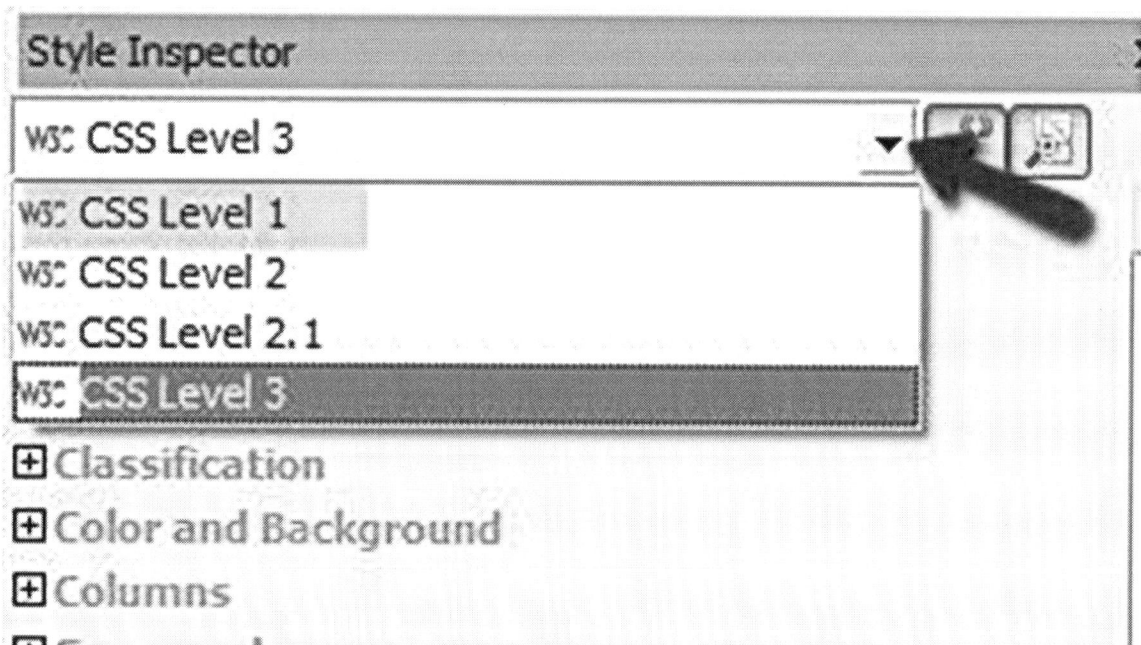

OK; now you should see far fewer categories, so let's get on.

We want to change the color of the h1 header font, so look for the category **Color and Background**.

Note: Each category is collapsible, so collapse them all first. Then open each one in turn to see what it contains.

OK, open the Color and Background category and select the color property. You will see a little artist's easel icon appear at the end of the line. Click on that easel and a color selector appears:

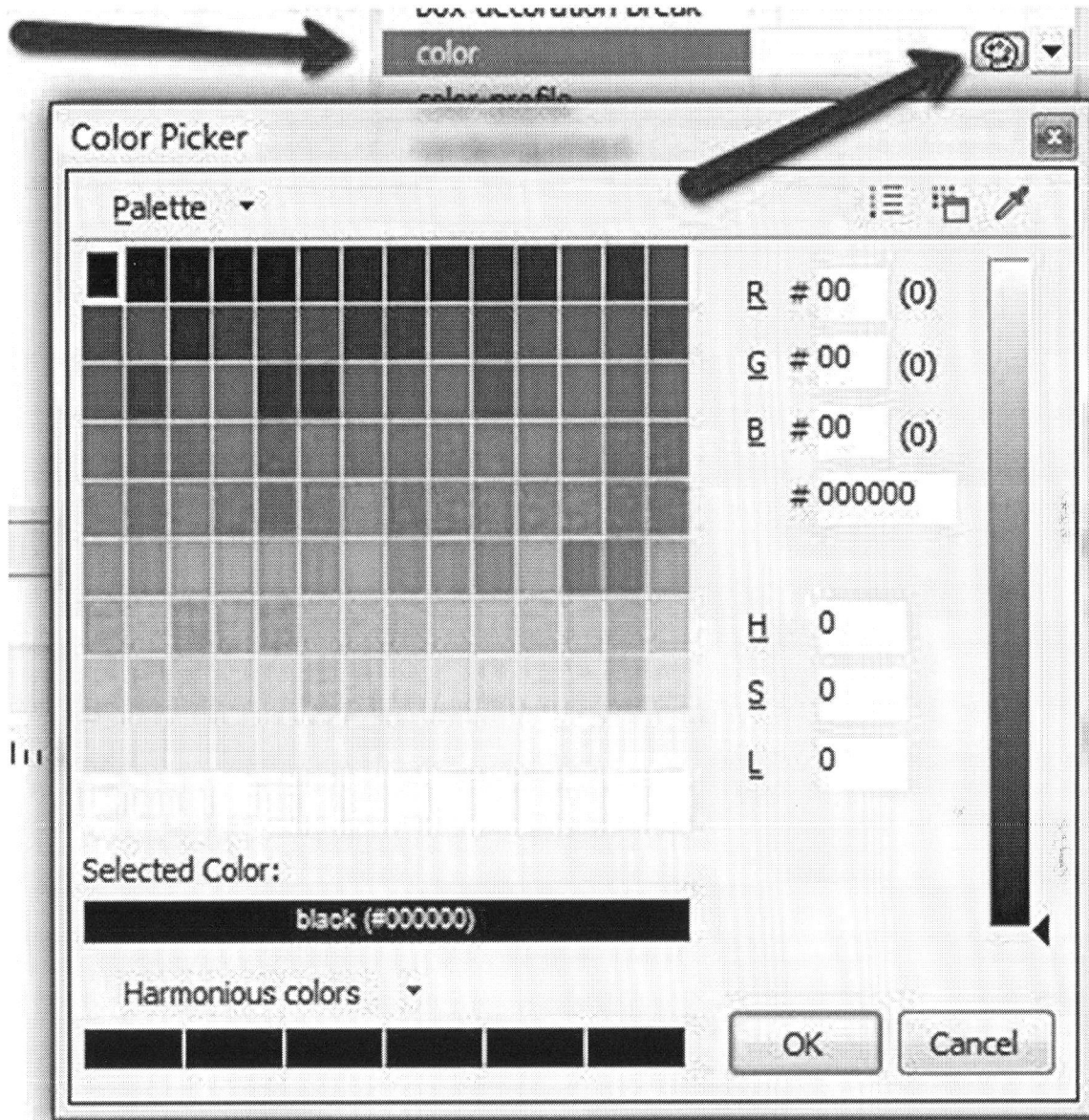

Simply select a color for your h1 header and click OK.

I've selected dark blue for mine:

```
2.3.css*  ✕
1 ⊟ h1 {
        color: #00008b;
     ⊢ }
```

You can see that the rule has been updated. The **hex code** (colors used in designing web pages), for my chosen color, now has a dark blue background so that I can easily see what color the code represents.

NOTE: If you are not using TopStyle, I will show you where you can get these hex codes for any color in a few moments.

OK, you will now see there is a preview of your H1 tag at the bottom of the main screen in the WYSIWYG (What You See Is What You Get), window.

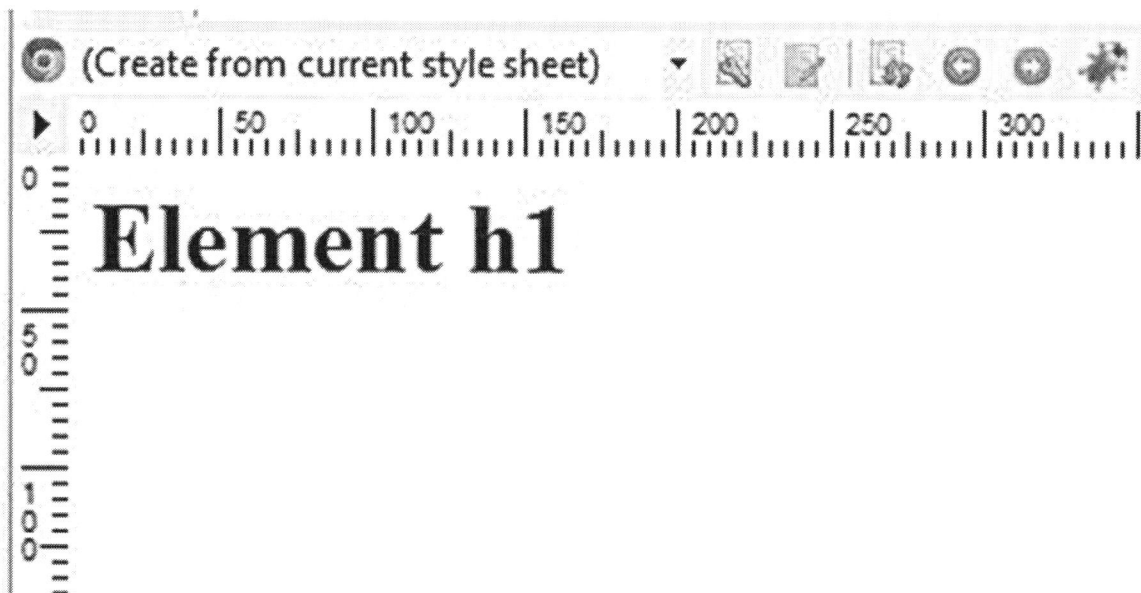

```
⊙ (Create from current style sheet)    ▾  🖾  📝  🖾  ⊙  ⊙  ✳
  ▶  0         50        100       150       200       250       300
0

   Element h1

5
0

1
0
0
```

I am not happy with this blue; so I want to make it lighter.

To edit the color, you can either click on the artist easel again, found on the right. Or you could just select the color property and the easel will reappear. Alternatively, you can right click the property inside the rule, and this will open a menu of options for you:

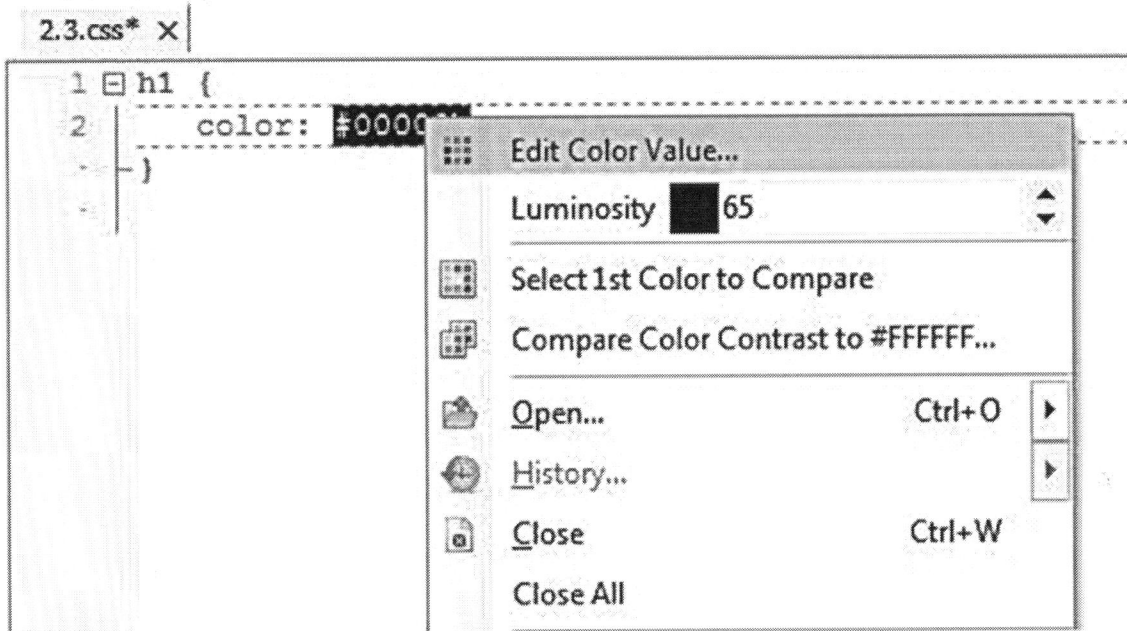

The top item in this menu is **Edit Color Value...** Click that and you will get the same color selector we saw before. Just select the color you want and click OK to update your style sheet.

If you are not using TopStyle to create your style sheet, you can choose your colors from here:

http://www.w3schools.com/tags/ref_colorpicker.asp

HTML Color Picker

Get darker/lighter shades of any color.

Select color: Darker/lighter shades: Hex values:

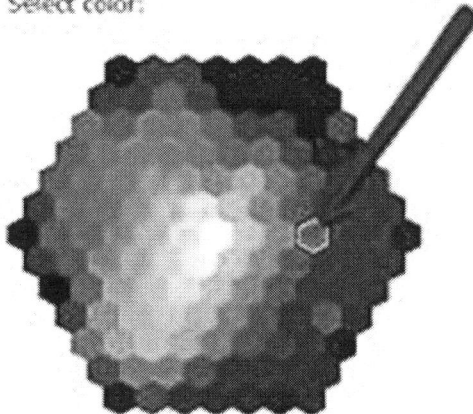

#000000
#1A0A1A
#331433
#4C1F4C
#662966
#803380
#993D99
#B247B2
#CC52CC
#E65CE6
#FF66FF
#FF75FF
#FF83FF
#FF94FF
#FFA3FF
#FFB2FF
#FFC2FF
#FFD1FF
#FFE0FF
#FFF0FF
#FFFFFF

#FF66FF

Selected color: [#FF66FF] [Submit]

Choose a color from the left hexagon. Then you have the different shades of that color on the right (see image). Next to each of these is the hex code. It is this code that you use in your style sheets.

You will notice that your style sheet will change to include your selected color.

38

Here is mine so far:

```
2.3.css  ☒

1 ⊟ h1 {
2 │     color: #0002db;
  │ └ }
```

Don't worry about the hex code **#0002db**. You do not need to remember any of these. This may not mean anything to you, but to web browsers it represents a fairly dark blue.

OK, now I want to make all H1 headers appear on a light blue background.

In the Style Inspector, look for the "background-color" property (again it's in the **Color and Background** category), and just select it.

Again, you can use the artist's easel to pick a color, but there is also a dropdown button with a simple color selector. It's on the right of the easel.

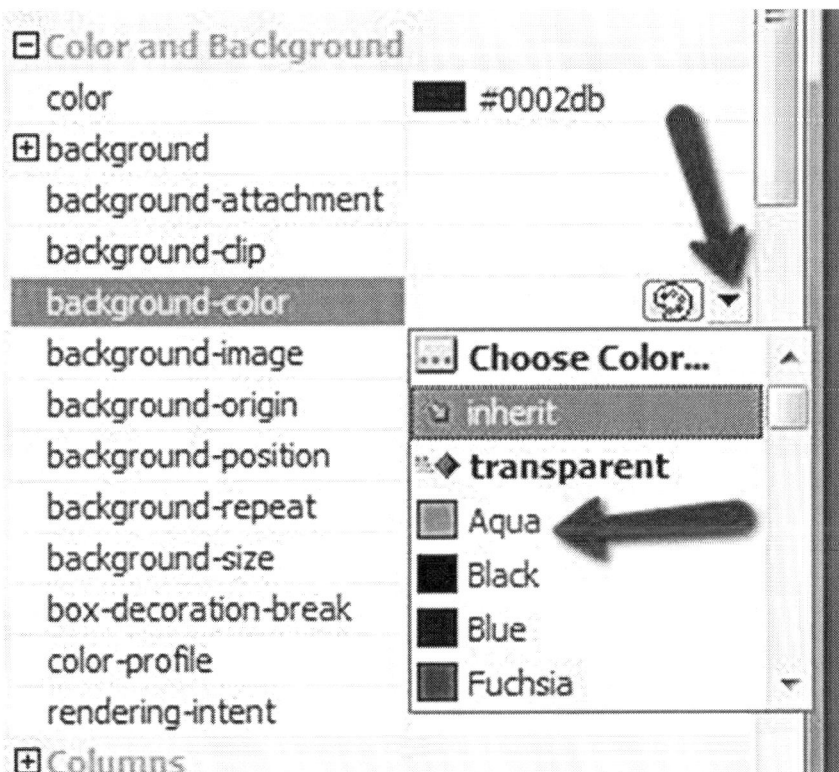

⊟ Color and Background
   color   ■ #0002db
⊞ background
   background-attachment
   background-clip
   background-color
   background-image   ... Choose Color...
   background-origin   inherit
   background-position   ◆ transparent
   background-repeat   □ Aqua
   background-size   ■ Black
   box-decoration-break   ■ Blue
   color-profile   ■ Fuchsia
   rendering-intent
⊞ Columns

I will use this color selector this time and just select **Aqua**.

Here is how my style sheet now looks for the h1:

```
h1 {   color: #0002db;
       background-color: aqua;
}
```

You can now see how this looks in the preview screen at the bottom of the TopStyle window. If you're not happy with it, you can simply modify the color and view the changes immediately.

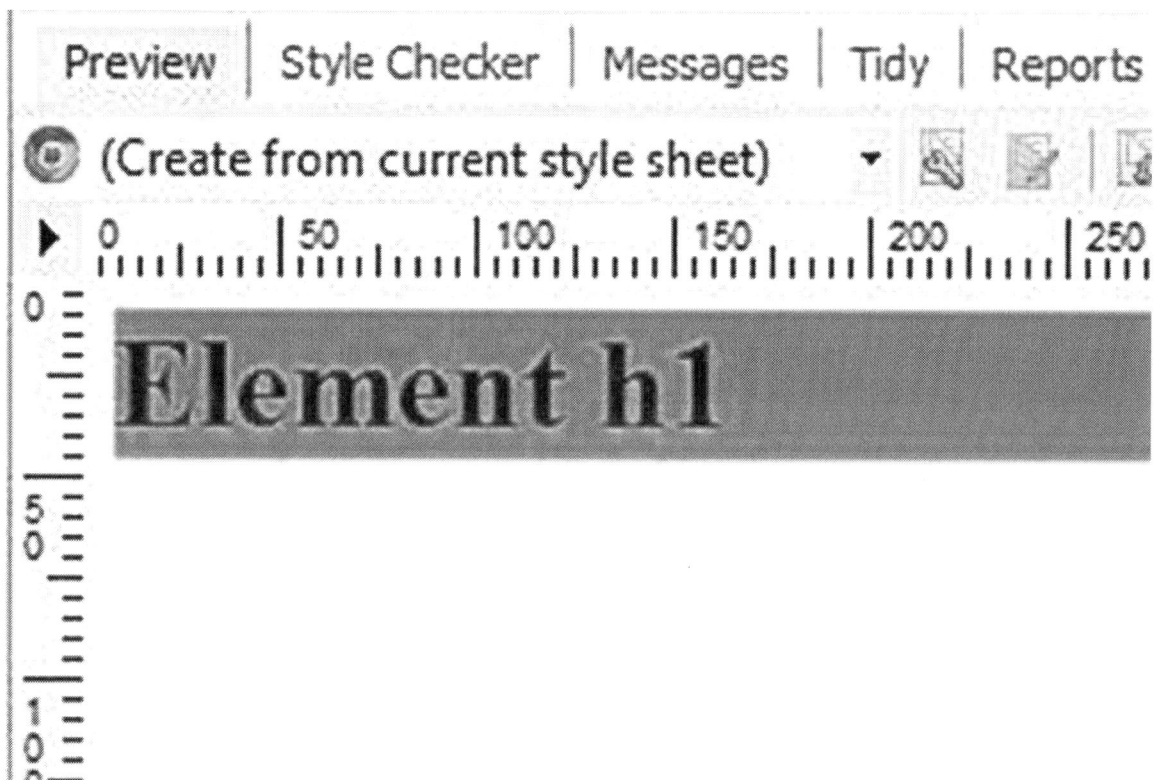

Let's now add a dotted border to our h1 headers. A border forms a "box" around the header, so the Inspector puts this property in the box category.

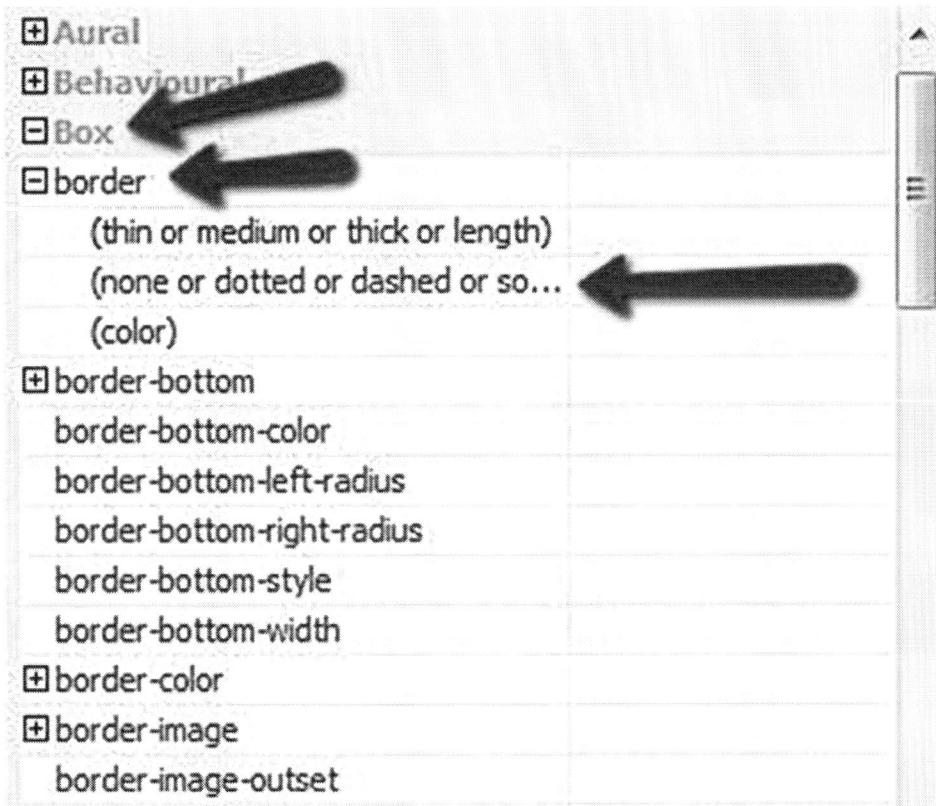

Open the box category and then click on the small + symbol next to the border property.

You now have some options. Click on each one to see what's available. To add the dotted box around the h1 header, we have to select 'dotted' from the (none or dotted or dashed or so...) property.

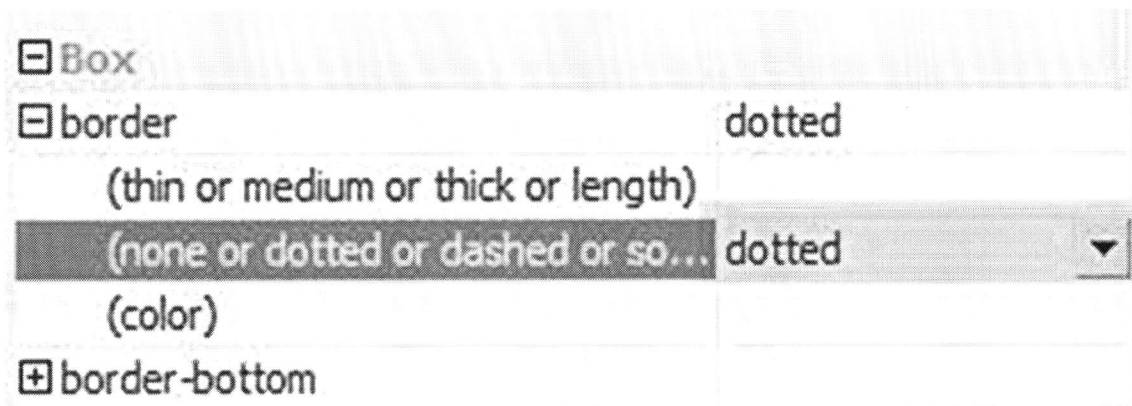

Notice that there is also a color property in with the border properties. This allows us to change the color of the dotted line. For this example, I will select a dark blue. When you're finished with yours, click 'OK' and your style sheet will be updated.

Here is how my new style sheet looks:

```
h1 {    color: #0002db;
        background-color: aqua;
        border: dotted navy;        }
```

One final change to this selector is to change the font.

Look for "font" in the inspector (clue: font is a category).

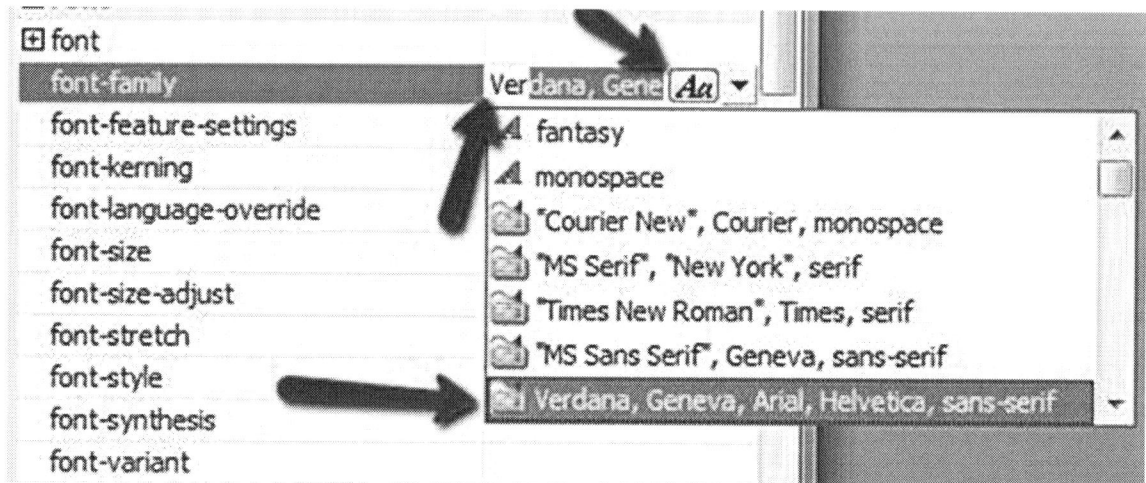

To the right of **Font Family**, you can start typing in the font family you want and it will appear in the box. Alternatively, you can click the "Font" button to dropdown the full list of fonts available.

I want the "**Verdana, Geneva, Arial, Helvetica**" font family. Basically this means that the web browser will try to use Verdana if it is on the computer, and if it's not, it'll then look for Geneva and so on.

When you start to type Verdana into the font-family box, that option appears right away, so just select it. When you click into the main style sheet section of the editor, your font family will appear in the property list. Here is mine:

```
h1 {    color: #0002db;
        background-color: aqua;
        border: dotted navy;
        font-family: Verdana, Geneva, Arial, Helvetica, sans-serif;  }
```

(2.3.css)

Notice how the preview window now changes to use your preferred font.

OK, I think you can play around with the h1 a bit more if you want to, and explore the various properties you can apply to this selector.

So what about other selectors; what else can we change the appearance of? Well, click the "New Selector" button again and then click on the "Simple" tab. You will now see the list of HTML elements available. These are all the possible selectors that you can define in your style sheet.

We will look at more of these in the next few sections of this course, but for now, let me identify two important selectors. You can then explore these on your own:

a – In HTML, a link is formed by using the <a></a> tag. Therefore if you create a rule for "a", you can control the appearance of links on your page.

*Note: This is the opening tag - <a> - and to close it, a forward slash '/' is used. So in this case it's </a>. All elements **must** have a closing tag otherwise they will not work.*

p – In HTML, the <p></p> is used to mark paragraphs. Therefore, adding rules for "p" will change the way your paragraphs look.

Using only the few selectors we have mentioned so far, you can dramatically change the appearance of a web site quickly, easily and effectively.

There are still a lot of selectors we haven't seen yet. Nevertheless, you should have enough information now to explore some of these CSS selectors, and their properties, and come up with your own basic style sheets.

I advise you to now create a few style sheets using the selectors that we have seen so far. If you want to create them in a text editor, you can, but you will need to use a reference source to identify which properties are available for each one. For that, I recommend this web site:

http://www.w3schools.com/cssref/css_selectors.asp

5. Pseudo Classes

In the last chapter we created a simple cascading style sheets (CSS). Hopefully you have had time to play around a bit, and become fairly comfortable with creating a style sheet.

One thing I can't do in this course is to teach you everything there is to know about CSS. There's just too much, plus it's a constantly evolving language. So my goal here is to get you up and running, and up to a point where you can be confident to go off on your own and learn more as necessary.

CSS contains a lot of technical terms, and I don't want to confuse you with them. Having said this, it is important to use the correct terminologies so that you don't get confused when reading other sources of information.

One of these terms I need to cover is "pseudo classes".

Basically a "pseudo class" can modify the appearance of a selector, depending on the "state" of that selector.

OK, so what does that mean in an 'easy-to-understand' language? Well, let's look at some examples, as this will help clarify the function of pseudo classes.

Open TopStyle and click on the "New Selector" button.

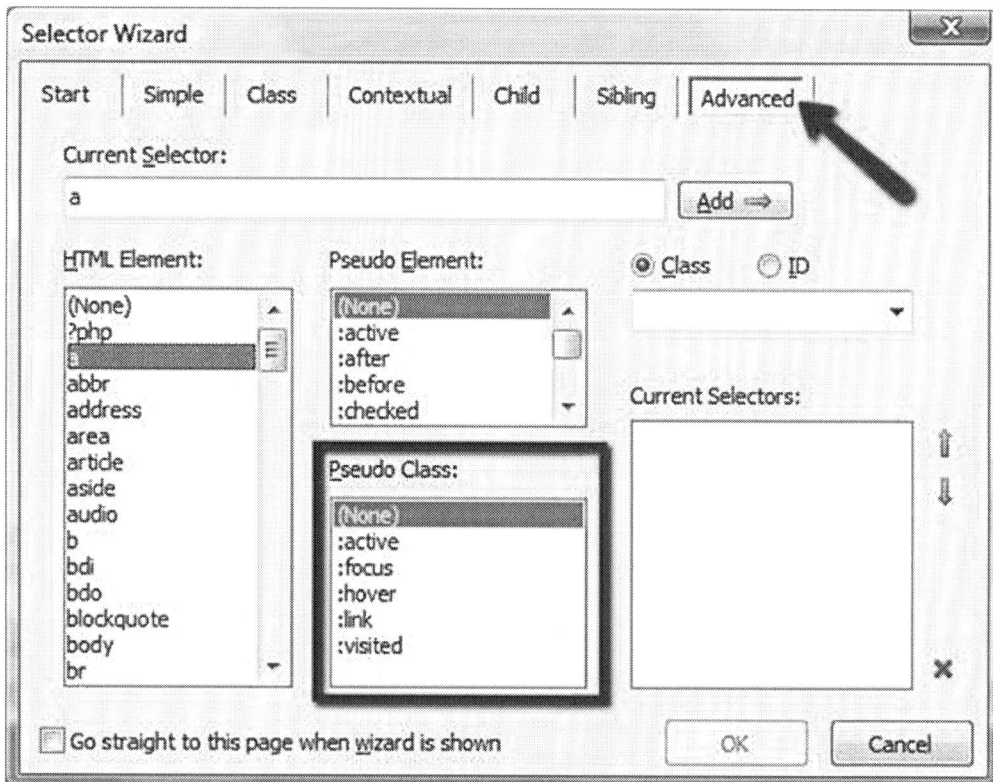

Next click on the "Advanced" tab located along the top right.

Now click in the HTML elements in the list on the left. Keep an eye on the Pseudo class box. If you scroll down the list of html elements, you'll notice that "a" is the only one that has pseudo classes.

Select "a" which as you now know refers to links.

Now look into the Pseudo Class box.

This lists the pseudo classes for the HTML element we have selected. The "a" tag has several pseudo classes which represent the "states" of a link on your page. The pseudo classes are as follows:

:active (refers to a selected link)

:focus (when an element has the focus, meaning it can accept keyboard input. We won't bother with this one, but it can be useful for say web forms, as it can highlight which box is accepting the input).

:hover (refers to a link when the cursor is hovering over it)

:link (refers to an unvisited link)

:visited (refers to a visited link, i.e., the appearance of a link after it's been clicked on by the visitor)

To use one of these pseudo classes is very straightforward. Just include it after the selector, for example, a:active, a:hover and so on. Fortunately this is very easy with TopStyle as it will create these for you.

IMPORTANT: You need to learn the order in which you MUST define these pseudo classes in your CSS file whenever you use them.

For them to be effective, you have to define them in the following order:

:link

:visited

:hover

:active

You don't have to use all of them, of course, but those you do use MUST be defined in this order in your CSS file.

OK, let's now create a style sheet that modifies the links on a page.

45

Here we're going to create a style sheet in TopStyle that defines all four of the above pseudo classes. To do this, start by following the screenshot below to form your link code:

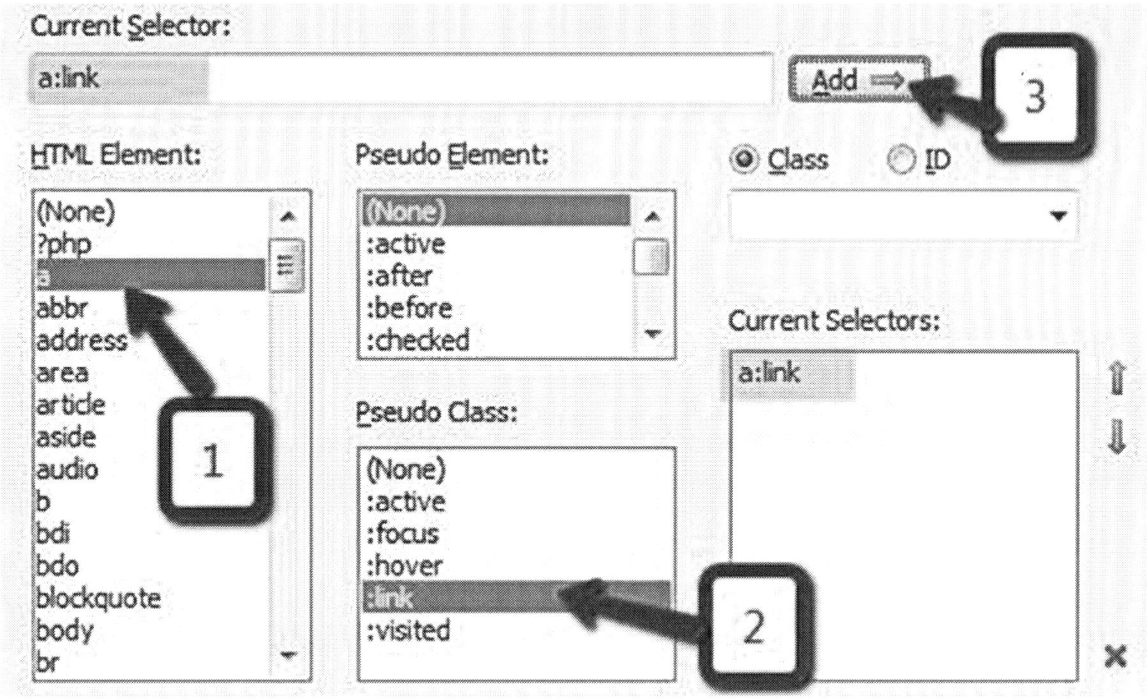

The written instructions for this are:

1. Select "a" from the HTML Element box.
2. Select ":link" from the pseudo class (you will notice that the **Current Selector** box top left changes to **a:link**).
3. Click the "Add" button. The selector now appears in the **Current Selectors** box on the lower right.
4. Click OK to add the Selector to the style sheet.
5. Repeat for **visited**, **hover** and **active** in that order.

Your style sheet should now look like this in the editor:

a:link {
}
a:visited {
}
a:hover {
}
a:active {
}

Remember, the order is very important to get the links to function properly.

NOTE: *You can add multiple Selectors at the same time simply by not clicking the "OK" button between each one. This way, they all appear in the Current Selectors box at the same time, like this:*

Current Selectors:

```
a:link
a:visited
a:hover
a:active
```

OK   Cancel

The resulting Style sheet looks like this:

```
a:link, a:visited, a:hover, a:active {
}
```

You only do this if you want to assign the exact same properties (the stuff that goes inside the curly brackets) to ALL of the states.

OK, it's time to have some fun.

Let's set the font-families property for each of the pseudo classes. Start by positioning your cursor inside the curly brackets belonging to the **a:link** selector.

On the right, find the category **Fonts** and open it up by clicking on the small **+**. Inside you'll find the font-families property.

Click on the button on the right with the capital "A" followed by the small "a" (**Aa**). This is the font selector button and it will give you a dropdown list of the available fonts. To find the "font-families", click on the small button at the bottom right, located just above the "Cancel" button.

Now click on the font family we want to use (in this case, the Courier one at the top), and click OK. You style sheet should now be updated with the font-families so that it looks like this:

a:link {

       font-family: "Courier New", Courier, monospace;

}

Repeat this procedure for each of the other pseudo classes, but choose a different font family for each one.

Here is what my completed CSS file looks like:

```
a:link {
        font-family: "Courier New", Courier, monospace;
}
a:visited {
        font-family: "MS Serif", "New York", serif;
}
a:hover {
        font-family: "Times New Roman", Times, serif;
}
a:active {
        font-family: Arial, Helvetica, sans-serif;
}
```

And this is what my links look like with this style sheet:

This page shows three links with a modified font-family

ezSEONews

Creating Fat Content

Google

(5.1.html & 5.1.css)

All three links look the same right now because they are all unfollowed links, and therefore have the font described in the a:link selector.

So what happens if I move my mouse over one of the links?

Well, when the a:hover selector comes into play, the font for that link will change to the properties specified in the a:hover selector, in this case that's the font-family: "Times New Roman", Times, serif:

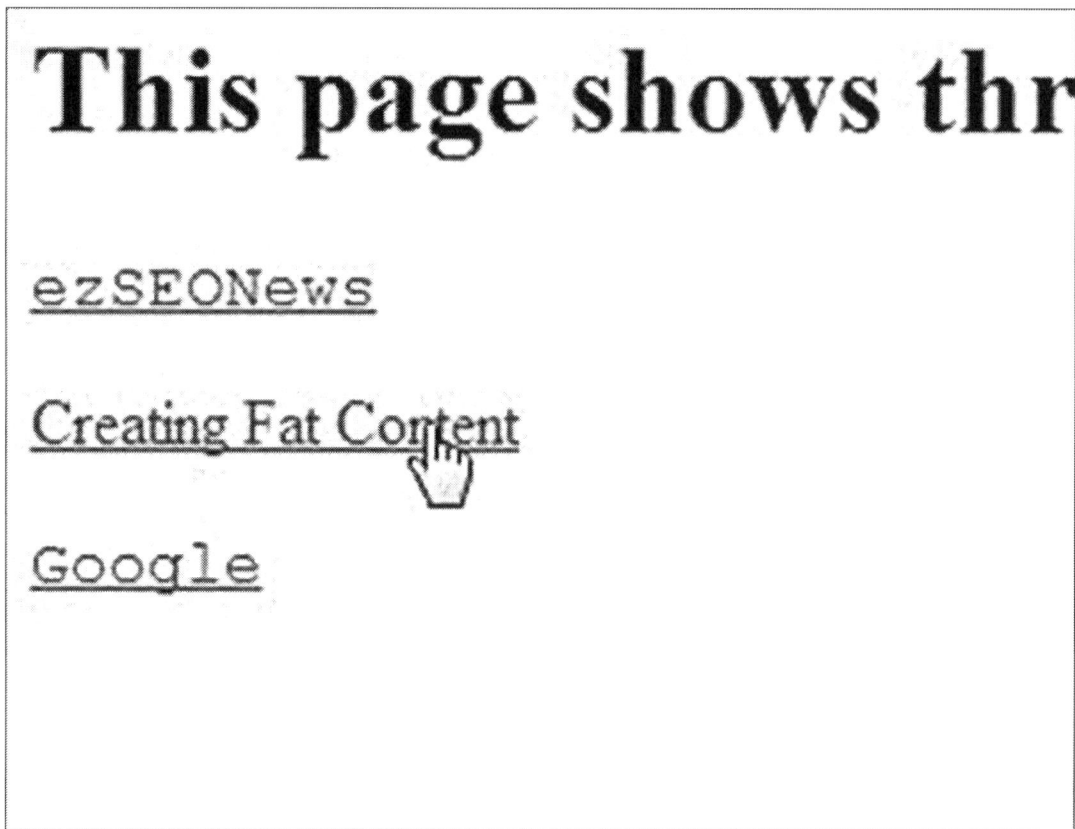

If I clicked on one of the links, and then came back to this page, the a:visited properties would be used to show the link has been followed, or clicked on.

Now, clearly we don't want different font families for each "state" of the link. Let's go into the editor and change the style sheet so that ALL links have the same font family. You can directly edit the style sheet in the editor. Just copy the font-family declaration from the first one and then paste it into each of the others. This is how mine looks now:

a:link { font-family: "Courier New", Courier, monospace; }

a:visited { font-family: "Courier New", Courier, monospace; }

a:hover { font-family: "Courier New", Courier, monospace; }

a:active { font-family: "Courier New", Courier, monospace; }

NOTE: To save space I have put each selector onto a single line. Remember, white space is not important.

What's more usual with links that are hovered over by the mouse cursor is to add an effect of sorts. This might be something like a change in color, an underline, or some other visual effect that tells the visitor the link is there. Hover effects can also encourage users to click-through.

Let's make the background-color yellow when the cursor moves over it, and also add a blue border to the top of the link.

First click inside the curly brackets of the **a:hover** pseudo class. Now on the right, find the Box category, and select the top-border property. You will see the border-top can be expanded by clicking on the "+" sign.

In the border-top-style property, select a solid line.

In the border-top-color property, select a blue color.

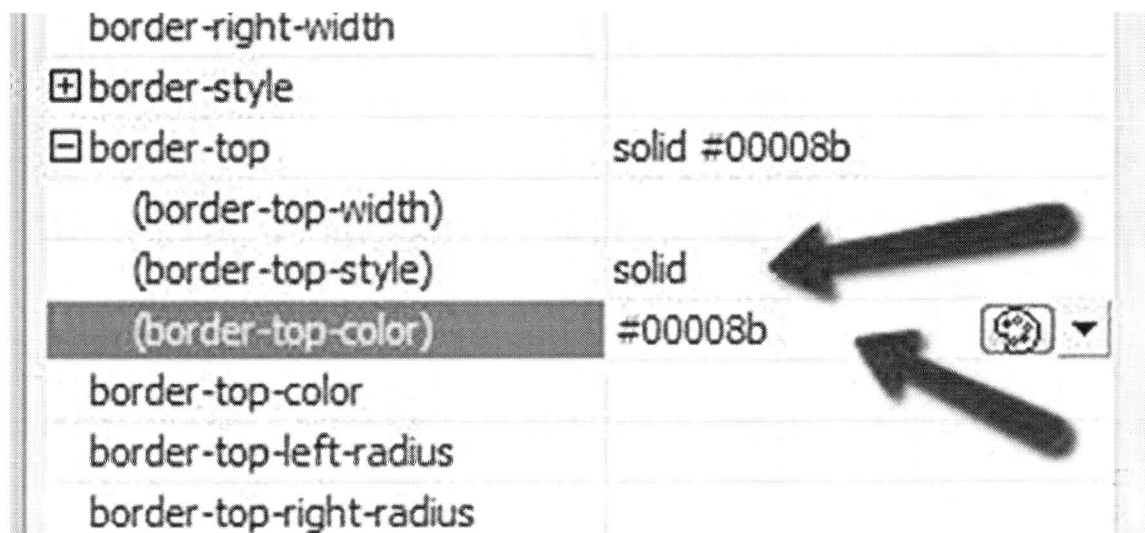

Here is my new a:hover rule:

a:hover { font-family: "Courier New", Courier, monospace; border-top: solid #00008b; }

We still need to make the background-color yellow, so let's do that and see what it looks like.

Look for the **Color and Background** category in the Style Inspector. In there you will find the background-color property.

Select a yellow for this:

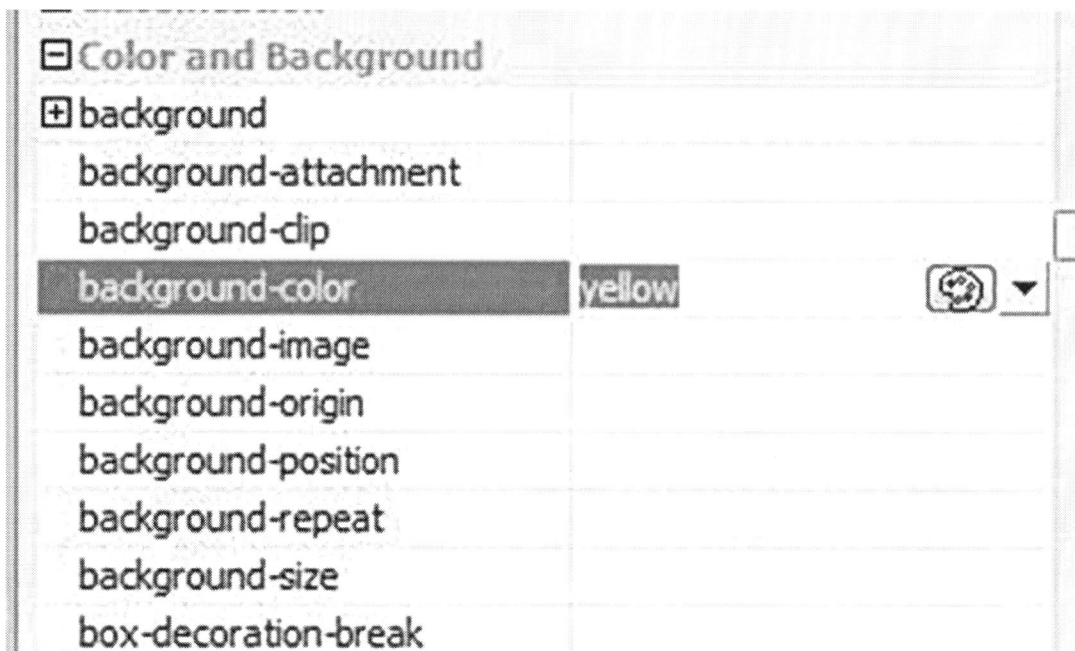

OK, so my final a:hover pseudo class now looks like this:

a:hover { font-family: "Courier New", Courier, monospace; border-top: solid #00008b; background-color: yellow; }

Let's see what this hover effect looks like on a web page.

This page shows th

ezSEONews

Creating Fat Content

Google

(5.2.html and 5.2.css)

As you can see, when I hover (position), my mouse cursor over the link, it changes to match the a:hover properties we have just created.

You might like to make that top border line thinner so that it matches the underline. You can do this by changing the border-top-width (inside border-top) to "thin". I won't do that for you. Have a go yourself. I'll be right here when you get back!

OK, let's now change the appearance of links that have been visited. For this, we need to modify the **a:visited** pseudo class.

In this example, I will change the font color of visited links to a dark grey.

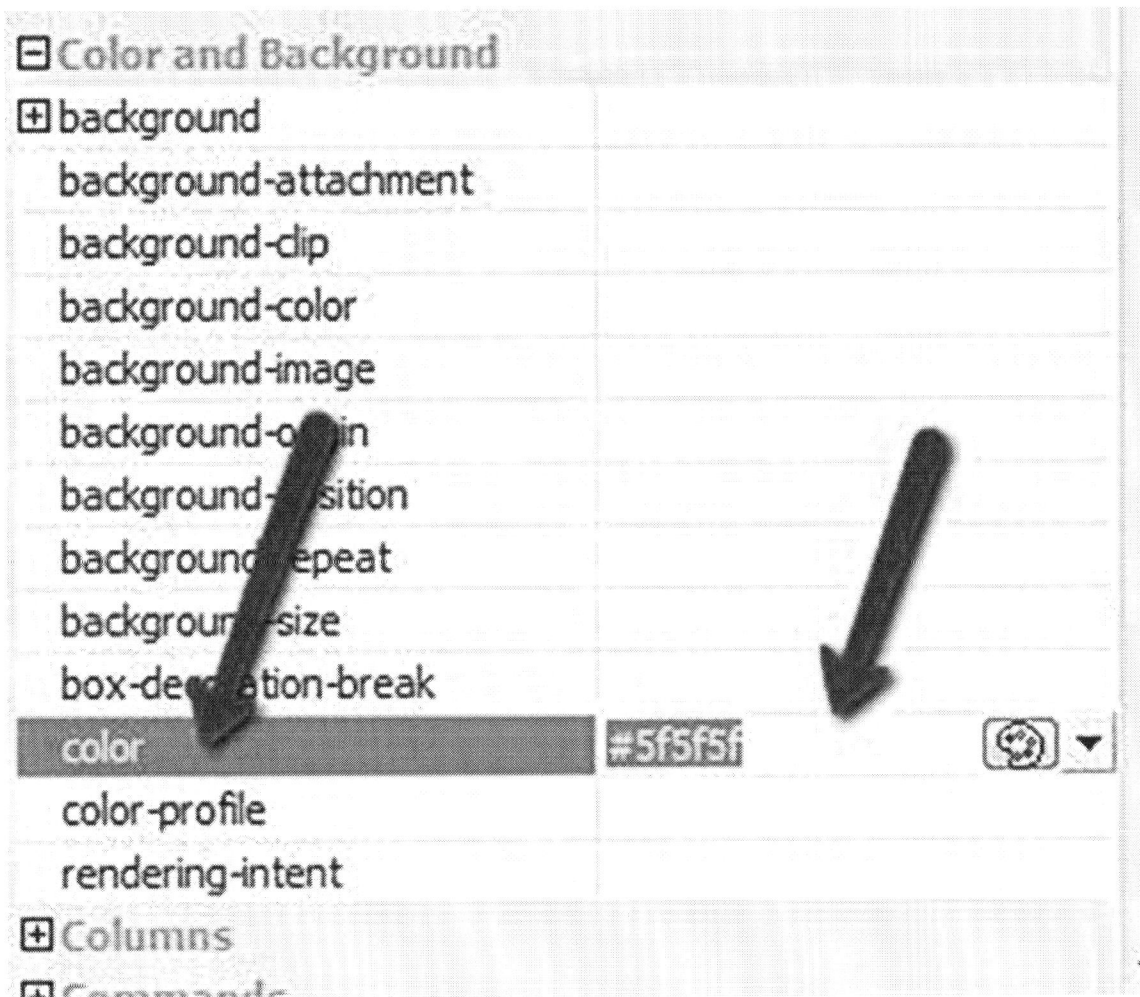

In the Color and Background category, look for color and select a dark grey.

This page shows tl

ezSEONews

Creating Fat Content

Google

(5.3.htm & 5.3.css)

See how the Google link (which I clicked before revisiting the page), has changed to grey? The browser now knows to use the style we have created using the a:visited properties for visited links. This is useful for visitors because it shows them which part(s) of a website they have already visited.

OK, we still have one pseudo class that we haven't used yet – **a:active**.

So just what is the a:active pseudo class for? Well, a link becomes active (displays some special effect), when you click on it. I don't actually expect you will use this pseudo-class much as it doesn't always behave as predicted, and will depend on the browser you use as to how it behaves, or not, as the case may be.

I have added a property to my a:active pseudo class to make the background red when a link is active. You can check this effect in any browsers you have on your computer to see how the link reacts.

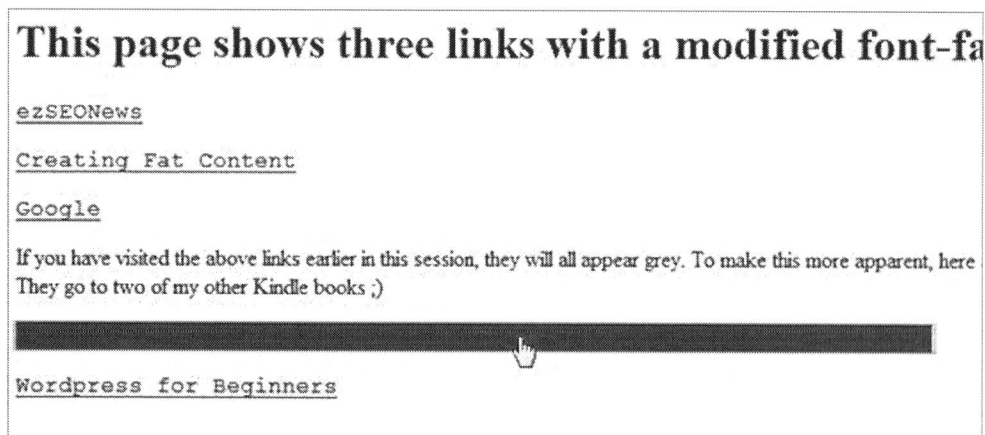

This page shows three links with a modified font-fa

ezSEONews

Creating Fat Content

Google

If you have visited the above links earlier in this session, they will all appear grey. To make this more apparent, here
They go to two of my other Kindle books ;)

Wordpress for Beginners

(5.4.htm & 5.4.css)

When I click on the link in the Google Chrome web browser, you see the red background, and releasing the click removes the color.

Experiment with these pseudo classes at your leisure. You should be able to see how **link**, **hover** and **visited** can make your website links more intuitive for visitors. These are the pseudo classes you typically see on the majority of web pages, simply because they're the most useful ones for site visitors.

OK, while we were going through this section, you may have noticed another window in TopStyle labeled **Pseudo Elements**. Let's now have a look at those.

6. Pseudo-Elements

Don't be put off by the name, pseudo-elements are not that difficult.

Let's start off with an example:

If you have ever had problems identifying niches, or you build a site that you think will be pr
has opened up a new site (it's called a membership site, but it is a one-time payment only).
37 ways to identify hot niches, and check them for profitability.

I have had a look around the site, and have to say, there is a huge amount of information in t
covers other areas on affiliate marketing as well (with lots of great resources), but for anyo
you.

A lot of the information on the site is freely available on the web, but its conveniently pack
having said that its freely available, there are a lot of resources I have never seen before
certainly get good value out of this site.

All in all, this site is a great resource, and one I'll be using myself. Gary is continuing to ad
you're interested, get in now.

(6.1.html and 6.1.css)

Using Pseudo-Element selectors, I have modified the first letter of each paragraph to achieve a drop-capital effect.

In this tutorial, we will look at two of these pseudo-elements (there are others, but they are beyond the scope of this book):

1. :first-letter
2. :first-line

In our example above, we used the **first-letter** pseudo-element (pseudo meaning false, because there is no corresponding HTML tag or attribute that is being modified).

To do this yourself, first open TopStyle.

Create a new style sheet, and then click on the "new selector" button. Now go to the "Advanced" tab again.

Select "p" from the HTML element list.

You will now see that the "Pseudo-Element" box has some values inside.

Find and select "first-letter", and click the "Add" button, followed by OK to save it to the style sheet:

You can now see your style sheet has been updated, and looks like this:

p:first-letter {

}

This tells the web browser to apply the formatting found inside the brackets to the first letter of each new paragraph.

Note: Paragraphs are surrounded by <p></p> tags. However, it is possible to have text on your page that appears as a paragraph in your browser, but is not surrounded by these tags (see below).

For example, take a look at the third paragraph on this page:

If you have ever had problems identifying niches, or you build a site tl has opened up a new site (it's called a membership site, but it is a on 37 ways to identify hot niches, and check them for profitability.

I have had a look around the site, and have to say, there is a huge am covers other areas on affiliate marketing as well (with lots of great re yo

A lot of the information on the site is freely available on the web, but it: said that its freely available, there are a lot of resources I have never se good value out of this site.

All in all, this site is a great resource, and one I'll be using myself. G you're interested, get in now.

(6.2.html & 6.2.css)

Notice that the first letter is not altered. If you examine the source code of that page, you'll see that the "paragraph" has no <p> tags (unlike the others).

```
<body>
<p>If you have ever had problems identifying niches, or you build a
that you think will be profitable, and its not, then Gary Harvey mig
the answer. He has opened up a new site (it's called a membership si
it is a one-time payment only). Gary has done extensive research int
markets, and found 37 ways to identify hot niches, and check them fo
profitability.</p>

<p>I have had a look around the site, and have to say, there is a hu
amount of information in there. Not everything on the site is about
hot niches, as Gary covers other areas on affiliate marketing as wel
lots of great resources), but for anyone who has troubles identifyin
niches, this site will certainly help you. </p>

A lot of the information on the site is freely available on the web,
conveniently packaged into one site - a niche resource site, if you
However, having said that its freely available, there are a lot of r
I have never seen before (Gary has spent many hours researching and
compiling). I will certainly get good value out of this site.

<p>All in all, this site is a great resource, and one I'll be using
Gary is continuing to add new stuff all the time, and the price is d
up soon, so if you're interested, get in now.</p>
<p></p>
</body>
```

It is worth remembering this, because it highlights the importance of good HTML when building your website(s).

OK, let us now go back to TopStyle.

So we're going to change the font of the first letter. To do this, start by clicking inside the curly brackets of the **p:first-letter** properties.

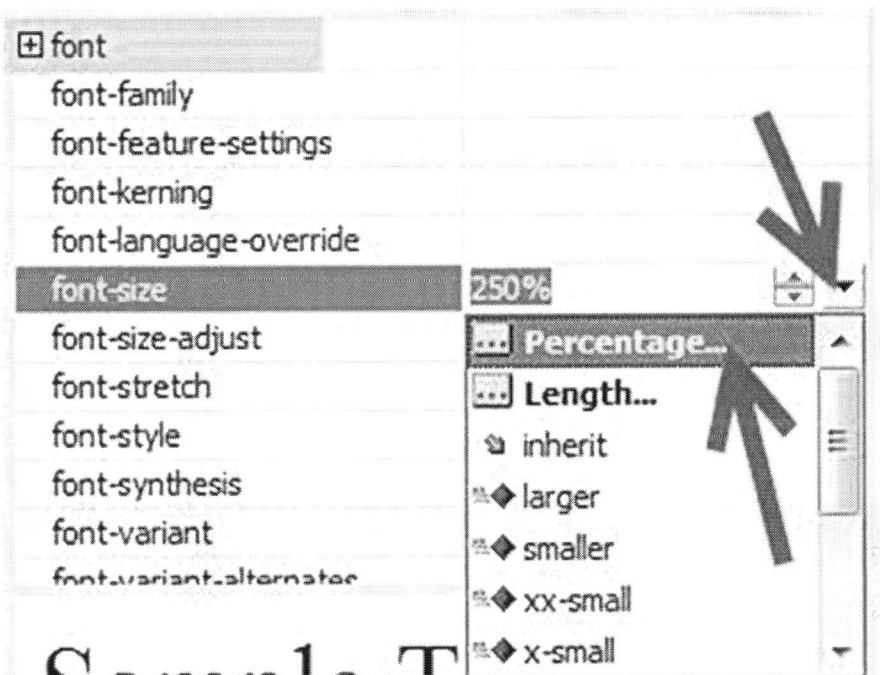

Look for the **Fonts** category in the Style Inspector, and click on the **font-size** option. Next, click on the downward arrow on the far right of this row and select **Percentage...** You will be asked to type in a value, so enter 250.

Your style sheet will update to look like this:

p:first-letter { font-size: 250%; }

You can now see the chosen effect in the preview at the bottom of TopStyle.

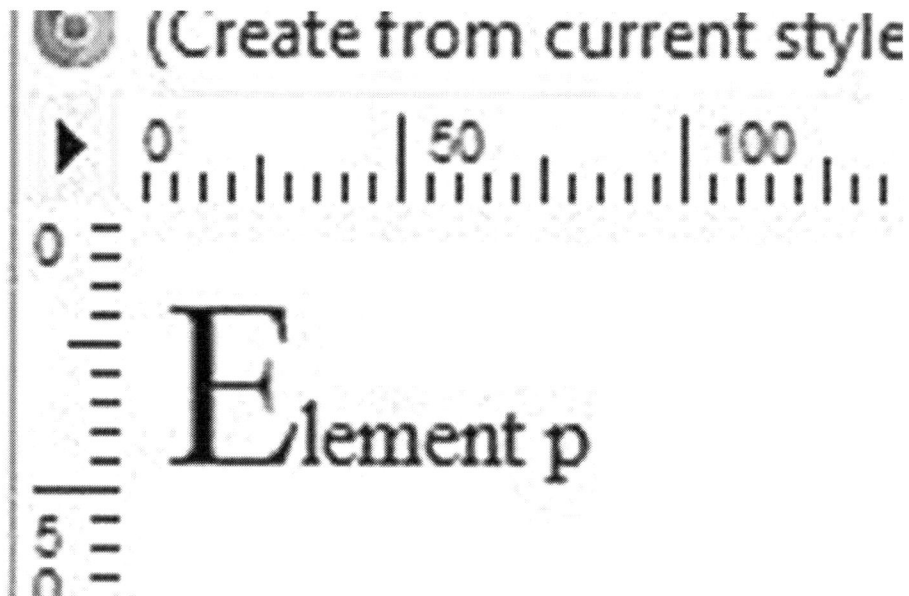

However, the capital letter is sitting on the same "line" as the rest of the text, and we want to drop it down. For this, we need to "float" the capital letter on the left hand side, so that the text will wrap around the first letter.

Once again, make sure you click inside the curly brackets of the selector you want to modify. We need to select the "float" property, and that is found inside the **box** category.

⊞ border-width		
box-align		
box-direction		
box-flex		
box-flex-group		
box-lines		
box-ordinal-group		
box-orient		
box-pack		
box-shadow		
clear		
float	left	▼
⊞ margin		
margin-bottom		
margin-left		

Click on it and then select **left** from the dropdown box.

Notice how the preview has changed? Your capital letter has now dropped below the line, and the rest of the paragraph wraps around it.

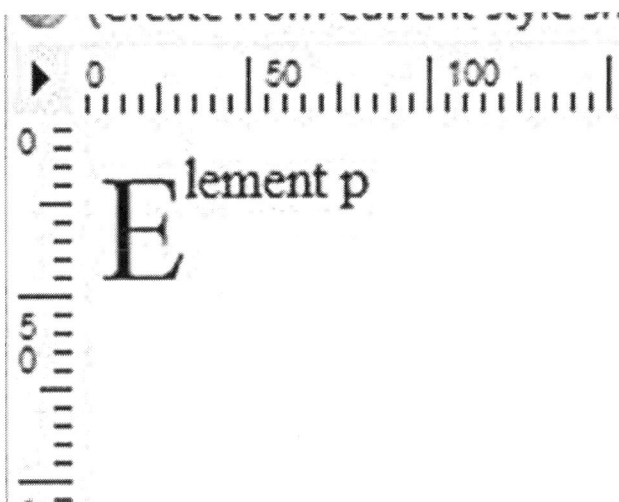

NOTE: You can use the "float" style with images too, to wrap text around them. You can also apply font styles and colors etc., to this selector, so have some fun. Here is the basic selector:

p:first-letter { font-size: 250%; float: left; }

61

You will also notice that other HTML elements can be modified with this **first-letter** pseudo element. Here is a page where I have modified the H1 header to change the font on the first letter of the headline:

(6.3.html and 6.3.css)

OK, I think you get the idea with this pseudo-element selector, and it's limited only by your imagination. But there's also the other one we mentioned, the "first-line", so let's take a look at that.

As the name implies, this modified the first line of the HTML element, and below is an example where I have modified only the first line of each paragraph:

(6.4.html and 6.4.css)

You have enough information now to play around with these two pseudo-elements, so I'll leave it there for this chapter.

Note: *You may find that certain browsers don't behave as you would expect them to when using these pseudo-elements. That brings us to one of the most important lessons in CSS, which is to cross-check browser compatibility BEFORE publishing your site.*

7. The "Float" Property

In the last chapter we looked at "Pseudo-Element Selectors", and despite its complicated name, we saw that they were in fact very easy to exploit.

The "drop-capital" example from the last chapter used the "float" property. It is that property I want to look at now, but with specific reference to images.

NOTE: If you use a very high screen resolution, then the examples given in this section may not show properly. Please resize your browser if necessary, so you can see the wrapping properly.

OK, here is the main problem. Have a look at this page:

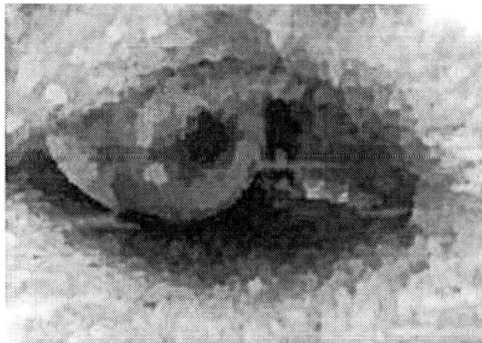

(7.1.html)

See how the text stops, and then we have an image, and then more text? Wouldn't it be better if the text flowed around the image instead? It would mean far less white space on the page, but more importantly, it just looks better. After all, creating a good impression for our site visitors is fundamental in web design.

Fortunately, CSS can do this for us. In the last chapter we used the float property to do just that with the "drop capital". Here we will do the same with images.

Take a look at this page:

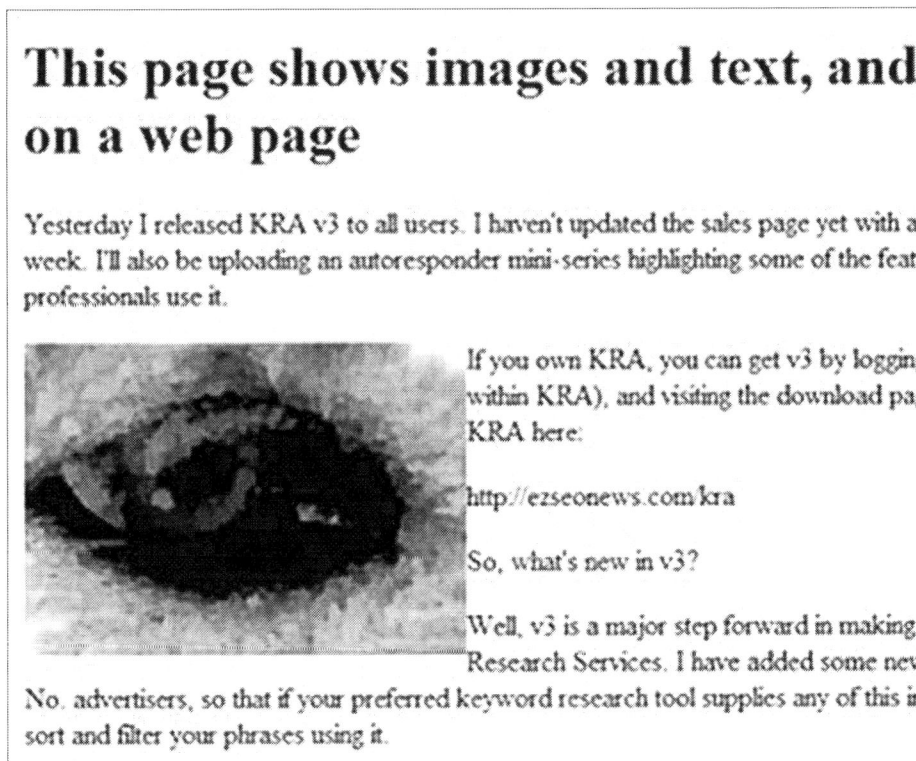

This page shows images and text, and on a web page

Yesterday I released KRA v3 to all users. I haven't updated the sales page yet with all week. I'll also be uploading an autoresponder mini-series highlighting some of the featu professionals use it.

If you own KRA, you can get v3 by logging within KRA), and visiting the download pag KRA here:

http://ezseonews.com/kra

So, what's new in v3?

Well, v3 is a major step forward in making Research Services. I have added some new

No. advertisers, so that if your preferred keyword research tool supplies any of this in sort and filter your phrases using it.

(7.2.html and 7.2.css)

See how the text now wraps around the image? Let's see how we did this.

Okay, so open TopStyle.

Create a new CSS file, and select the "New Selector" button. Click on the "Simple" tab, then find and select **img** in the HTML elements. Click on "Add" and then click OK to include it into your style sheet. You should now see this:

```
img {
}
```

Now, look down the **Style Inspector**, and find the "float" property inside the **Box** category. Select "left". Your style sheet should now look like this:

```
img { float: left; }
```

NOTE: You can float to the "right" as well. This simply means the image will be on the right of the screen and the text wrapped around on the left:

If you look at the last screenshot there are a couple of problems. The first drawback is that the text is too close to the image. I want a space between the image and the text so that it's easier on the eye.

Go down the **Style Inspector** and find the "margin" property (again in the **box** category). Open it if necessary by clicking on the small "+", and you'll see a "margin-right". Click the downward arrow to the right of this row, and select length. You'll be prompted with a dialogue box:

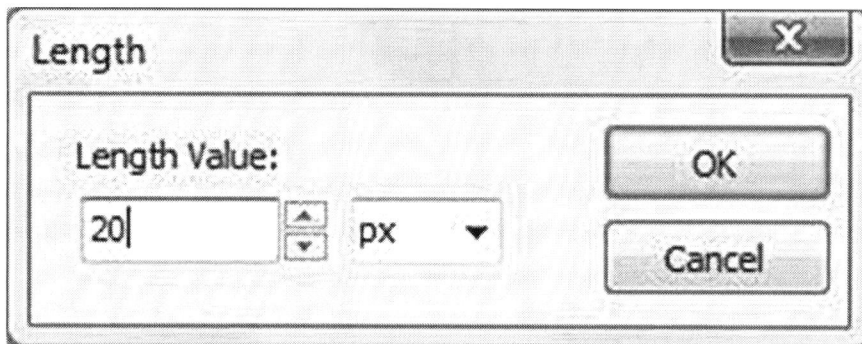

Length

Length Value:

20| px

OK

Cancel

Type in 20 and leave the measurement box set as px (pixels).

Your style sheet will now look like this:

img { float: left; margin-right: 20px; }

And this is what the web page now looks like (the colored highlight is only there to draw attention to the new space):

This page shows images and text on a web page

Yesterday I released KRA v3 to all users. I haven't updated the sales page week. I'll also be uploading an autoresponder mini-series highlighting sc professionals use it.

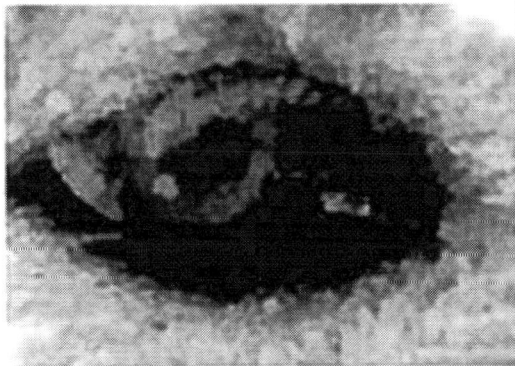

If you own KRA, you can within KRA), and visiting KRA here:

http://ezseonews.com/kra

So, what's new in v3?

Well, v3 is a major step f Research Services. I have Clicks, No. advertisers, so that if your preferred keyword research too then sort and filter your phrases using it.

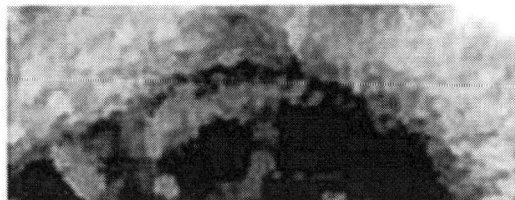

Another major addition is projects, and Import Prof want shown for each pro;

(7.3.html and 7.3.css)

You can also play around with the image "border" styles if you want to.

Here is an example where I have added a blue dashed border to the images:

(7.4.html and 7.4.css)

Here is the CSS for that:

img { float: left; margin-right: 20px; border: thin dashed Blue; }

Now, this is all well and good, but there is another problem. What if I don't want all of my images displayed in the same way. For example, what if I want some aligned right?

Well, CSS provides a solution for that too with Class & ID selectors (we will look at the difference between classes and IDs in a minute, so don't worry about that now). What these Class & ID selectors do is allow us to over-ride the display properties of individual HTML elements.

Have a look at this page:

This page shows how ID Selectors are used to apply styles to individual HTML elements.

Yesterday I released KRA v3 to all users. I haven't updated the sales page yet with all of the changes, but should be doing that this week. I'll also be uploading an autoresponder mini-series highlighting some of the features of KRA, showing why so many professionals use it.

If you own KRA, you can get v3 by logging into the customer site (via the help menu within KRA), and visiting the download page. For everyone else, you can read about KRA here:

http://ezseonews.com/kra

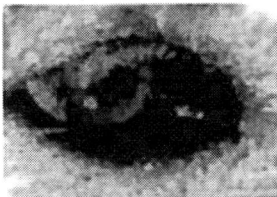

So, what's new in v3?

Well, v3 is a major step forward in making KRA compatible with a lot of Keyword Research Services. I have added some new data types: ratio, CPC, EPC, No. Clicks, No. advertisers, so that if your preferred keyword research tool supplies any of this information, you can now import it and then sort and filter your phrases using it.

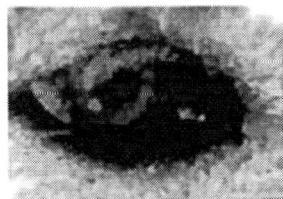

Another major addition is the addition of Option profiles, which can be "attached" to projects, and Import Profiles. This means that you can specify which bits of data you want shown for each project, and KRA will automatically adjust which data is shown for each project when opening the project.

Also, a much needed addition is the ability to export entire databases, or just filtered sets of a database, to a new project.

(7.5.html and 7.5.css)

I've aligned one image on the left, and the other on the right.

I basically created one CLASS to align my images right, and another CLASS to align my images left.

I appropriately named these classes as **rightalignimage,** and **leftalignimage.**

Now, whenever I want an image aligned left, I simply add the CLASS into the image HTML so the browser knows what it needs to look up in the style sheet.

Here is the HTML to insert an image into a webpage:

<img src="golfo.gif" >

(golfo.gif is the name of the image I am inserting).

And here is the HTML to insert a right-aligned image into my web page after defining the class in the style sheet:

<img **class="rightalignimage"** src="golfo.gif" >

I have highlighted the code that aligns my image to the right. This is just a reference to the rightalignimage CLASS.

Cool stuff eh?

NOTE: *You can call classes and Ids whatever you want, but they should be descriptive so you know what they do.*

If you are feeling a little lost with classes and Ids right now, don't panic! We are going to look at them in more detail in the next chapter.

8. IDs and Classes

In the last chapter we looked at Class & ID selectors, and I left you with this example:

This page shows how ID Selectors are used to apply styles to individual HTML elements.

Yesterday I released KRA v3 to all users. I haven't updated the sales page yet with all of the changes, but should be doing that this week. I'll also be uploading an autoresponder mini-series highlighting some of the features of KRA, showing why so many professionals use it.

If you own KRA, you can get v3 by logging into the customer site (via the help menu within KRA), and visiting the download page. For everyone else, you can read about KRA here:

http://ezseonews.com/kra

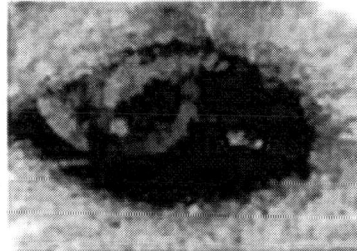

So, what's new in v3?

Well, v3 is a major step forward in making KRA compatible with a lot of Keyword Research Services. I have added some new data types: ratio, CPC, EPC, No. Clicks, No. advertisers, so that if your preferred keyword research tool supplies any of this information, you can now import it and then sort and filter your phrases using it.

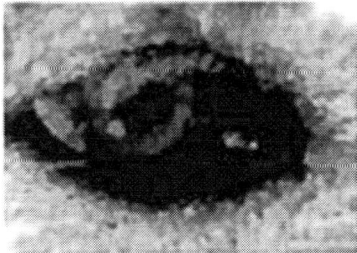

Another major addition is the addition of Option profiles, which can be "attached" to projects, and Import Profiles. This means that you can specify which bits of data you want shown for each project, and KRA will automatically adjust which data is shown for each project when opening the project.

Also, a much needed addition is the ability to export entire databases, or just filtered sets of a database, to a new project.

(7.5.html and 7.5.css)

In that illustration, I created a couple of classes to modify the properties of images. One for left align, and one for right align.

71

Now take a look at this page:

This page shows how ID Selectors are used to apply styles to individual HTML elements.

Ignoring the extra images, visually it looks very similar to the first page, doesn't it? The only difference here, is that instead of defining two classes, I defined two "ID"s.

Now, **this page breaks a major CSS rule** that I'll tell you about in a minute.

However, I have checked this webpage in a variety of popular web browsers, and you know what? No browser (except some very old ones), had a problem with the code, and they all showed the images alternating left to right.

NOTE: Firstly, and probably the most important lesson to learn is that web browsers vary in their support for CSS. In fact, as you continue working with CSS, you'll find that Internet Explorer is one of the worst culprits here. Therefore, it's important to check your web pages in various browsers BEFORE publishing them on the Internet; something that's overlooked by too many – unfortunately!

Another lesson to learn from this is that it is relatively easy to make a mistake in your CSS, especially if you start working with "cascading" style sheets. We also saw in an earlier part of this book that the order of selectors can be important. You therefore have a lot to remember, and the best thing to do is validate your web page to make sure there are no errors.

Here is the best place to validate your HTML:

http://validator.w3.org/

I recommend you always check your pages here.

When checking the web page that breaks the rule I mentioned, it informs me of several errors like these two:

> ❌ *Line 23, Column 13*: **ID "LEFTALIGNIMAGE" already defined**
>
> `<p><img id="leftalignimage" src="smilie.jpg"></p>`
>
> An "id" is a unique identifier. Each time this attribute is used in a document it must have a different value. If you are using this attribute as a hook for style sheets it may be more appropriate to use classes (which group elements) than id (which are used to identify exactly one element).

> ❌ *Line 19, Column 13*: **ID "RIGHTALIGNIMAGE" already defined**
>
> `<p><img id="rightalignimage" src="smilie.jpg"></p>`
>
> An "id" is a unique identifier. Each time this attribute is used in a document it must have a different value. If you are using this attribute as a hook for style sheets it may be more appropriate to use classes (which group elements) than id (which are used to identify exactly one element).

These two errors are a direct result of the incorrect CSS that I used to align the images on the webpage.

OK, the rule I mentioned is as follows:

ID selectors can only (or should only), be used **ONCE** on a web page, and identify **ONE** item on the page.

By using an ID selector to reference two images on the page, I was breaking a CSS rule. I should have used a CLASS instead.

ID Selectors and classes do essentially the same thing, BUT, **an ID can only be used once on the page**, whereas **classes can be used multiple times**.

Before we look at classes, let me give you an easy way to remember this:

Your ID refers to YOU and you alone. No one else can have your ID.

A class is a group of people, so a class can refer to multiple individuals.

Therefore, an ID is only used once, and a class can be used multiple times.

For this reason, we will use IDs for page elements that only occur once, e.g., when we come to look at page layouts using CSS, we'll define IDs for the page header area, the right and left margins, the main content section, and the footer. These are obvious choices, since each of those sections only occurs once per page.

We will use classes whenever we want to reuse a style on a page more than once, for example, the alignment of images, font styling, and bullet points, etc.

OK, we know that IDs and Classes can be used to override default display properties, but we still haven't looked at how to create or use them yet. Let's look at that now, so that you can start using them in your page designs.

8.1. ID Selectors

Start TopStyle and click on the "New Selector" button.

Switch to the "advanced" tab, and you will see a pair of radio buttons (aka option buttons), labeled Class and ID.

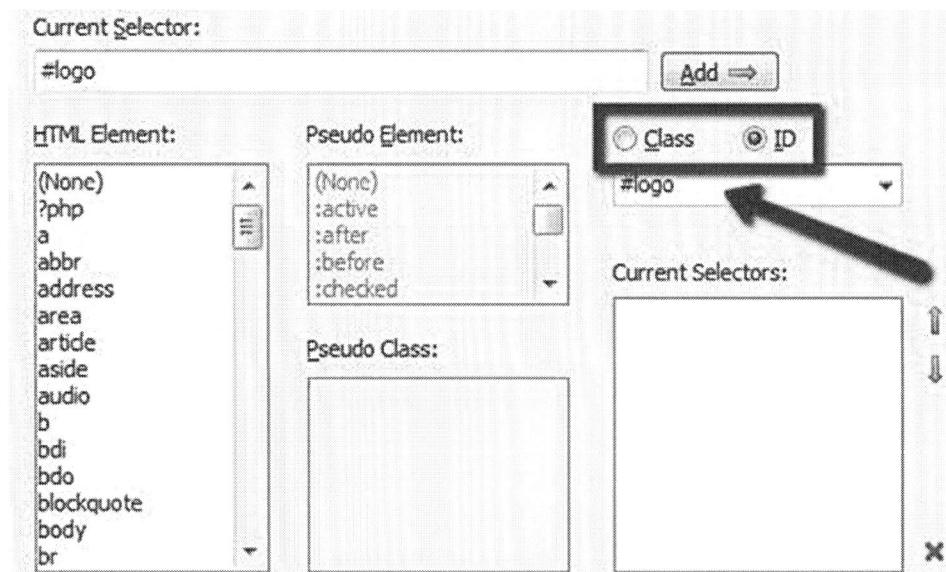

Select ID, and then in the box underneath the radio buttons, type in a name for your ID. I typed in "logo" for mine, since I am going to create the ID to be applied to the logo on the page (it only appears once).

You will notice that as you type, TopStyle adds a '#' to the start of your ID. Click the "Add" button (located above the radio buttons), and then click the "OK" button on the bottom right. This will add this selector to your style sheet.

In style sheets, the '#' symbol specifies that what follows is an ID. Here's how mind looks:

```
#logo {

}
```

You can now add some styles to the ID in exactly the same way we have done in other examples. I've added a few to mine, and here the finished logo ID:

```
#logo {
        font-size: 3em;
        font-variant: small-caps;
        font-weight: bolder;
        background-color: Silver;
        font-family: Verdana, Geneva, Arial, Helvetica, sans-serif;
}
```

The idea of this ID is to change the text properties in the logo area of my page so that it is larger ("em" is a unit of measurement that I will cover in chapter 9). My sample here uses small caps, bold, has a silver background, and is the Verdana, Geneva... font family. You probably knew this from seeing the style sheet though, didn't you?

You can see the effects of what this does to the page here:

> # Mylogo.com
>
> # This page demonstrates the use of an ID.
>
> Start Topstyle Lite, and click on the "New Selector" button.
>
> You'll see a pair of radio buttons labelled Class and ID. Select ID, and then, in the box underneath the radio buttons, type in a name for your ID. I am going to type in "logo" for mine, since I am going to create the ID to

(8.1.html and 8.1.css)

To use the ID in a web page, you simply modify the HTML tag to include:

ID = "logo"

Here is the HTML code before modifying:

<p>Mylogo.com</p>

Just before the first single right-pointing angle quotation mark ">", is where you insert your ID code:

<p **ID="logo"**>Mylogo.com</p>

Now, anything inside the <p></p> tags will be formatted according to the properties of the ID "logo".

You will notice that in the raw HTML, the text is lowercase apart from the first letter "M". In the web page preview (above), the text is small capitals, or small caps. That is what happens when we add the property: **font-variant: small-caps;**

Classes are used in a very similar way, so let's now take a look at that:

8.2. Class Selectors

Create a new style sheet, and click on the "New Selector" button. Go to the "Advanced" tab again and click on the "Class" radio button. Enter a name for your class underneath the radio button. I am using "yellowhighlight" for mine, as that is what my class will do. i.e., highlight some text in yellow.

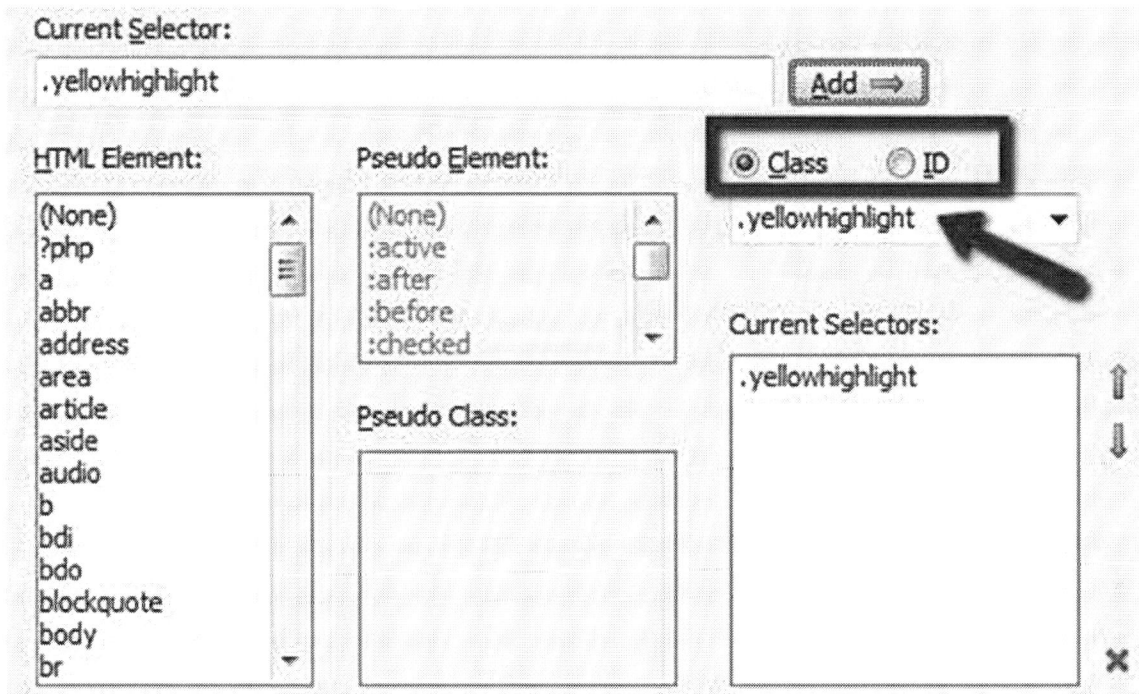

You'll notice that as you type, TopStyle adds a "." in front of the text you are typing. In CSS, that "." specifies that whatever follows is a class.

OK, once done, click the "Add" button and then click "OK" to save the changes to your style sheet.

This is what mine looks like:

```
.yellowhighlight {
}
```

I will make just one style change to the background color:

```
.yellowhighlight { background-color: Yellow; }
```

Now I can simply highlight a paragraph in yellow by adding the following code to the HTML tag for the paragraph I want to change:

```
class="yellowhighlight"
```

We add it in the exact same way that we added the ID earlier. Insert it right after the first ">" of the <p> tag.

Here is the html code:

```
<p class="yellowhighlight">the paragraph goes here</p>
```

77

Now look at this page:

MYLOGO.COM

This page demonstrates the use of an ID.

Start Topstyle Lite, and click on the "New Selector" button.

You'll see a pair of radio buttons labelled Class and ID. Select ID, and then, in the box underneath the radio buttons, type in a name for your ID. I am going to type in "logo" for mine, since I am going to create the ID to be applied to the logo on the page (it only appears once).

You will notice that as you type, Topstyle adds a '#' to the start of your ID.

In style sheets, the '#' denotes that what follows is an ID.

OK, name typed in?

(8.2.html and 8.2.css)

The second paragraph is now highlighted in yellow. Note how the <p> tag has been modified from <p> to <p **class = "yellowhighlight"**>:

Here is the HTML.

```
<body>
<p ID = "logo">Mylogo.com</p>
<h1>This page demonstrates the use of an ID.</h1>
<p>Start Topstyle Lite, and click on the &quot;New Selector&quot;
<p class = "yellowhighlight">You'll see a pair of radio buttons la
<p>You will notice that as you type, Topstyle adds a '#' to the st
<p>In style sheets, the '#' denotes that what follows is an ID.</p
<p>OK, name typed in? </p>
<p>Click OK, and your style sheet will be updated as follows:</p>
<p>#logo {<br>
  }<br>
</p>
```

Because I used a class to define the highlighting, I can happily use it on multiple paragraphs if I want to:

MYLOGO.COM

This page demonstrates the use of an ID.

Start Topstyle Lite, and click on the "New Selector" button.

You'll see a pair of radio buttons labelled Class and ID. Select ID, and then, in the box underneath the radio buttons, type in a name for your ID. I am going to type in "logo" for mine, since I am going to create the ID to be applied to the logo on the page (it only appears once).

You will notice that as you type, Topstyle adds a '#' to the start of your ID.

In style sheets, the '#' denotes that what follows is an ID.

OK, name typed in?

Click OK, and your style sheet will be updated as follows:

```
#logo {
}
```

(8.3.html and 8.3.css)

That's how easy it is to define and use classes.

Before we leave this though, I can hear you asking: "But what if we only want to highlight certain text in a paragraph, and not the whole section?"

Well, the problem here is that the way we have used the class so far is to modify a complete HTML tag (the whole paragraph), because we declared the class within the <p> tag.

However, there is another option. You can use a "span" tag, to surround a selection of text, and apply a class only to the "spanned" text. To do this, you have to surround the text you want to highlight with a <span></span> tag. Let's look at an example:

<p>I only want to highlight <span>this text</span>here.</p>

We can now add the class within the opening <span> tag, right before the ">", in much the same way as you saw previously with the other tags:

<p>I only want to highlight <span class="yellowhighlight">this text </span>here.</p>

Here it is in action on a web page:

Start Topstyle Lite, and click on the "New Selector" button.

You'll see a pair of radio buttons labelled Class and ID. Select ID, and then, in the box underneath the radio buttons, type in a name for your ID. I am going to type in "logo" for mine, since I am going to create the ID to be applied to the logo on the page (it only appears once).

You will notice that as you type, Topstyle adds a '#' to the start of your ID.

(8.4.html and 8.4.css)

This chapter is an important part of the CSS course, with some big lessons to learn. We learnt how to use IDs and Classes to modify the elements of our web pages, and although there's still more to cover on classes, we'll take a break for now. In the next chapter we will look at a confusing aspect of CSS, and that is the units of length.

9. Length Units

As you have followed this tutorial, you may have noticed that when you change the size of text using CSS, there are a number of options.

You can see this for yourself in TopStyle.

Create a new style sheet, and click the "New Selector" button. Select the "Simple" tab and select **h1** from the HTML elements list. Next click the "Add" button, followed by "OK".

In the style inspector, scroll down to the font category and click on the font-size property. Click the downward arrow on the right of this row to view the options available:

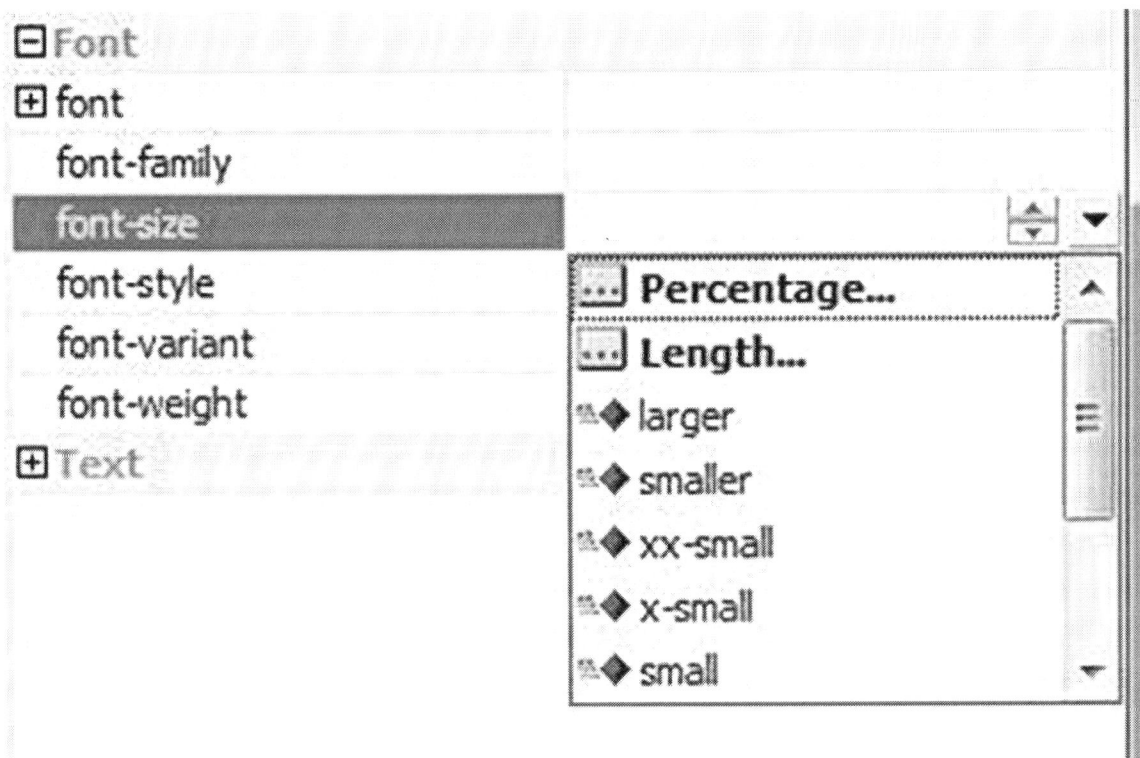

In this book, we will concentrate on the first two items in this list – **Percentage** and **Length**.

Percentage is a relative measurement (i.e., it defines a size that is relative to another one).

Length is an absolute measurement, since it defines an exact measurement. However, with exact measurements come units.

What are the units for an absolute measurement?

Well, let's find out. Click on the font-size dropdown arrow, and select length.

Another dialogue box opens up, with another dropdown box (set to the default 'px').

Click on the down arrow of that dropdown box, and you'll see several more options:

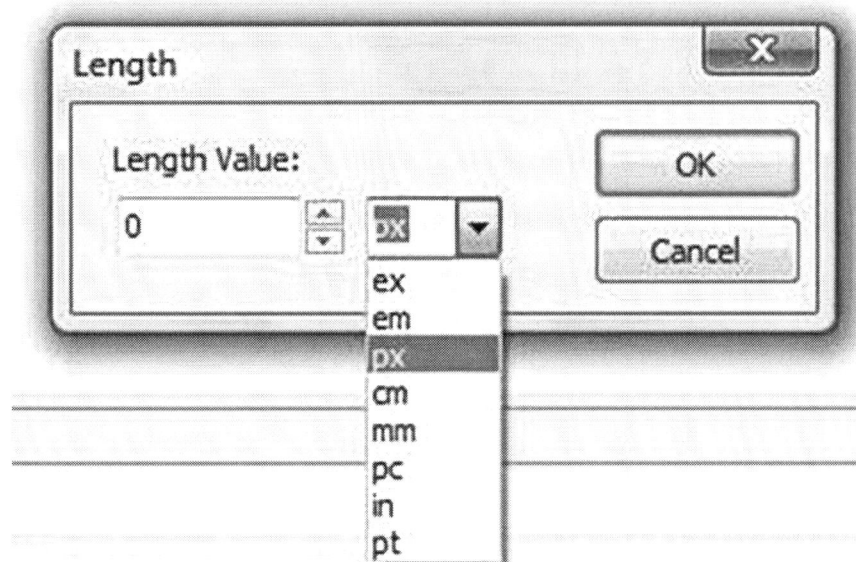

WOW! That's a lot of different units.

These units can be divided into two groups:

1. **relative units** (size is relative to something)
2. **absolute units** (size is an exact measurement)

The 'relative' units are:

- ex
- em
- px

(The percentage unit is also relative).

The 'absolute' units are:

- cm
- mm
- pc
- in
- pt

The main reason for using absolute units is to freeze the design of the web page so that it always looks the same, no matter how it's viewed.

When relative measurements are used, the web design may look different, depending on the users Web browser settings.

Let's look at an example.

This header uses an RELATIVE measurement to define its size.

This header uses a ABSOLUTE measurement to define its size.

There are two headers, one defined in absolute terms, and the other in relative terms.

Older web browsers use to allow users to change the size of the fonts in their browsers to:

- Largest
- Larger
- Medium
- Smaller
- Smallest

The problem was that any font size defined in absolute terms would not increase in size because it was set in absolute measurements, and therefore would always appear the same size on the screen. The font size defined in relative terms *would* increase in size.

If you increased the font size to "Largest", you'd see the relative header increase in size while the absolute header would stay at the same size.

To some extent, web browsers have taken away the functionality of absolute measurements because they introduced a zoom feature instead of a font size feature. This then magnified all text, absolute or relative, to the same extent, throwing out some web designer's carefully designed layouts.

OK, let's consider the units for measurements, and what they represent.

The five absolute measurements are as follows:

1. **cm** - centimeters
2. **mm** - millimeters

3. **in** - inches
4. **pc** - picas (1/6 inch or 12 points)
5. **pt** - points (1/72 inch)

It should be noted that even if absolute measurements did work properly in browsers with the new zoom features, they would only ever work as desired *if* the browser knew the size of the screen, and the number of pixels the screen displayed. In many cases, the browser would have to guess! This, together with the more recent addition of zoom features, means that absolute measurements aren't the best units to use when designing your pages, so we won't be looking into these.

It was important to mention absolute measurements in this book though, because I am sure you will come across them when you are exploring the CSS of your own (and other people's) web pages.

So relative measurements provide us with the best solution, especially when we don't know what device the end user will be viewing the site on. For example, nowadays they could be browsing on a computer, a tablet, a Smartphone, or even some e-readers. With relative measurements, the font sizes will be relative to the size of the screen, and therefore give the user the very best viewing experience.

Here are the relative measurements in some detail:

9.1. EX

The 'ex' is a measurement relative to the size of the font's lowercase 'x'. I never use this measurement, so we won't be looking at it in this book.

9.2. PX

The px is a relative measurement in screen pixels.

Pixels offer the designer the best control over layouts. You will see them used a lot for things like borders, margins, padding, plus height and width of screen regions when creating CSS layouts without tables (something we will look at later in this series).

What pixels are not recommended for is text size. Most modern browser won't have a problem, but some of the older ones won't resize pixel-based text.

9.3. Percentage

Percentage measurements are always relative to another value. For example, if we want to increase the spacing between lines of a paragraph, you can define the line-height as a percentage (it will be a percentage of the font size).

Say for example we have: line-height: 150%. This will create a space between the lines that is 150% of the font size. Therefore, if the font size is 10px, then the space between lines will be 15px. It is wise to define the font-size in your CSS file if using percentages, otherwise results can be unpredictable in the different browsers. This is because the font-size will be taken from the web browsers default CSS file.

Here is an example showing line spacing using percentages:

A normal Paragraph:

px- relative measurement in screen pixels. Pixels offer the designer the best control borders, margins, padding, plus height and width of screen regions when creating C this series). What pixels are not recommended for is text size. Some browser wont friend Internet Explorer wont resize pixel based text. Therefore, to give the best ex pixels.

A paragraph where lines are spaced at 150% (line-height:150%):

px- relative measurement in screen pixels. Pixels offer the designer the best control borders, margins, padding, plus height and width of screen regions when creating C this series). What pixels are not recommended for is text size. Some browser wont friend Internet Explorer wont resize pixel based text. Therefore, to give the best ex pixels.

A paragraph where lines are spaced at 200% (line-height:200%):

px- relative measurement in screen pixels. Pixels offer the designer the best control

borders, margins, padding, plus height and width of screen regions when creating C

this series). What pixels are not recommended for is text size. Some browser wont

friend Internet Explorer wont resize pixel based text. Therefore, to give the best ex

pixels.

(9.1.html and 9.1.css)

9.4. EM

The "em" is a relative measurement for the font size. Think of it as being the size of a capital "M" to help you remember it, though that isn't quite accurate, but it is a good way to memorize it.

This is my preferred unit for defining text size. Because it's a measurement relative to the font size, if we define a font-size of say 10px, then one em is equal to 10px. 2 em would be equal to 20px, and 1.5 em would be 15 px.

To make this as easy as possible, it's a good idea to define the font size in the style sheet as follows:

Create a new style sheet.

Click on the "New Selector" button, and then go to the "Simple" tab.

Select **body** from the HTML Element list, and then click the "Add" button followed by "OK".

You'll see the following in your style sheet:

body {
}

Whatever properties you enter will be the default properties for *all* elements on the page that appear between the <body></body> tags, i.e., everything.

I can define a default font-size like this:

body { font-size: 11px; }

This would make the default font size 11px. Here is a web page where I have defined the default text size in this manner:

This is a normal paragraph - Since I have not defined a size for <p> tags in the style sheet, it appears as 1em.

H1 header defined as 2.5 em

H2 header defined as 2 em

H3 header defined as 1.5 em

(9.2.html and 9.2.css)

In some older browsers, if you choose a larger font size, these sizes will remain the same because we defined the default font as 20 px – an absolute measurement. However, since most browsers now use the zoom feature, this is less of a problem that it used to be. Nevertheless, just to be safe, we are probably better off defining the default font-size this way:

body { font-size: 0.7em; }

This would make the default text size 70% of the default text size. So just what is the default text size?

Well, every browser has its own default CSS that it uses to display web pages. If you want to see what that size looks like in different browsers, create a style sheet that sets the body text size to 1em.

body { font-size: 1.0em; }

Then create a web page with some text on it that uses the style sheet, and view it in a few different browsers, or just look at 9.3.html and 9.3.css, as I have done this for you.

Here is a great article on using em for sizing text. Richard Rutter uses percentages instead of em to define the default font-size:

http://clagnut.com/blog/348

10. DIVs

We have come a long way in our understanding of CSS, and I hope I haven't lost you so far.

In this section, I don't want you to worry about what we are doing, or how it's done. Just sit back, and look at the examples. Study the HTML and the CSS if you want (no obligation), and enjoy the ride we are about to embark on. The how and why will come in the next few chapters of this book.

Here, I want to talk about a very useful "tool: in CSS design - divisions.

These divisions, or "<div> elements", are used to mark out regions of a page, or define regions of your HTML document that you want to treat as a unit. You can create a division element by using the following code:

ENTER YOUR CODE TO BE CONTAINED IN THE "REGION" HERE.

So why would we want to mark out regions of our document using < div> tags?

Well, imagine being able to apply a class or ID to a specific region of your web page. For example, envisage you are creating the header area for your front page, and you want the header text to by white on a black background. You can define a header region using DIVs and then set the properties of that DIV accordingly with CSS.

Have a think about these examples:

EXAMPLE 1 - How about marking some text and an image inside div tags, and then applying a border to the div element. The image and text would then be enclosed in a box.

How would you do that in HTML without using tables (which is one of the good reasons to use CSS in the first place, as tables bloat code and slow down the page load time)?

EXAMPLE 2 - How about defining a block of code inside a div, e.g., a menu, and then have that div float on the right hand side of the page?

EXAMPLE 3 - How about an AdSense rectangle code enclosed in a div, and then position that div top left of your main page content, with page content flowing around it. Sound good?

Have a look at this example:

Divs – mark our regions of your page

(10.1.html and 10.1.css)

Load that example in your browser and then resize the browser.

I have included an image and some text inside a div, and then set the property of the div to float right, plus made the background color bright green, and the border a darker, dashed green line.

You could also use something similar to enclose a menu that floats on the right of your web page, as another example.

Can you see the power of divs and CSS to help arrange the layout your pages?

Look at the next example. Here I've marked out two regions of the page using divs, and assigned one as a right-sided box, and the other, a left-sided box.

Divs - mark our regions of your page

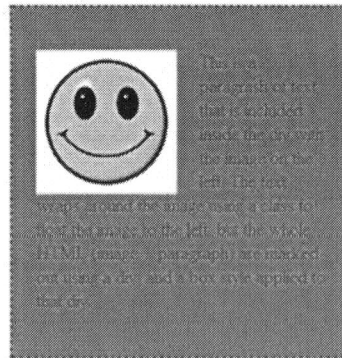

(10.2.html and 10.2.css)

Look at the source code of this example and then open the HTML document in your web browser and try to resize that browser.

Imagine creating a left and right hand menu instead of my images and text, and you should start getting excited at the potential here.

And how about this next example, where I have defined an area at the top of the page to hold the headline:

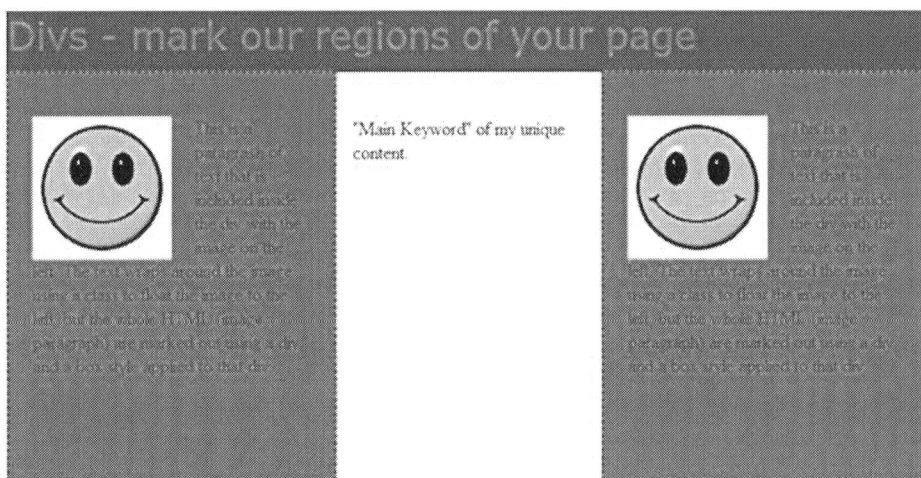

(10.3.html and 10.3.css)

What we are doing here is using DIVs to define regions (or boxes), of our page which will be placed at certain positions on the page. We are actually creating a webpage layout WITHOUT THE USE OF TABLES.

In that last example, I even added in a bit of main page content (text). To do this, I defined a region of the page with a DIV, and inserted my main page content in there. Feel free to examine the source code of both the HTML and CSS file.

Take a look at the HTML by viewing the source code of the document.

```
<body>

    <div id="main">"Main Keyword" of my unique co

    <div id="header">Divs - mark our regions of y

<div id = "boxr">
    <p><img class="leftalignimage" src="smilie.jp
    <p>This is a paragrash of text that is includ
    wraps around the image using a class to float
    paragraph) are marked out using a div, and a ]
    </div>


<div id = "boxl">
    <p><img class="leftalignimage" src="smilie.jp
    <p>This is a paragrash of text that is includ
    wraps around the image using a class to float
    paragraph) are marked out using a div, and a ]
    </div>
```

Notice how the DIVs are not in the same order as on the rendered web page?

The main DIV is before the header DIV. We can do this because the positioning of these DIVs on the page is controlled by the CSS file and not by the HTML document.

CSS is great for page layouts.

All of this is probably a bit confusing for you right now, but don't be discouraged. In the next chapter, we will start looking at how you can do all of this by yourself, in baby steps of course, until you manage to build a few CSS layout templates that can be used on your new site(s).

11. Creating a Simple 2 Column Layout

In the last chapter we saw some sample layouts, but I didn't go into any real details on how to achieve them yourself. This is what we are going to be doing now, and I promise, we will take it slowly.

The fixed-width layout - e.g., you can create a design that is 790 pixels wide. That means the site will always be displayed at 790 pixels wide, no matter what screen resolution the user is viewing it at. Obviously when viewed at higher screen resolutions, the web page will show smaller on the display, and at lower resolutions, it will appear larger. At a screen resolution of 640 x 480, the user will require scroll bars to view the whole page as it is then too big to fit into their browser window.

The liquid layout - web pages with a liquid layout will expand and contract to fill the browser. These are typically created by defining measurements in percentages, e.g., 100% of screen width. That means the web page will fill 100% of the screen, no matter what screen resolution the user is viewing at.

The elastic layout - this is a more complex design, and not one we are going to look at in this tutorial. Here we will concentrate only on the first two types of layout.

The first is a simple two-column layout. It is wise to draw out your design before you attempt to code it. Here is my two-column layout:

I have given relevant names to each of my areas on the plan. Every region is going to be created using IDs. But before we tackle that though, let's look at how we can create a single area.

OK, so open up TopStyle, and create a new CSS file.

Let's now create an ID called "leftmenu".

Click on the "New Selector" button, and go to the "Advanced" tab. Select the "ID" radio button (default selected is class).

In the box underneath, type "leftmenu" (without quotes).

Click "Add" followed by "OK", and your style sheet should now look like this:

```
#leftmenu {
}
```

Save the style sheet as **styles.css** to a folder on your computer.

In the same folder, create a simple web page, and add the following code to it:

```
<div id="leftmenu"> Contents go here </div>
```

All we have done here is to define "**Contents go here**" inside div tags (which we looked at earlier). We have assigned the ID "leftmenu" to everything inside those div tags. We haven't yet added any properties to the leftmenu ID in our style sheet, meaning right now the web page just contains those three words, so nothing fancy – yet!

Right before the </head> tag, add this line of code to call the style sheet:

```
<link rel="stylesheet" href="styles.css" type="text/css">
```

This will make sure that the style sheet is called on by the browser so that it can get the page formatting that "we" set.

(11.1.html and 11.1.css)

OK, let's now edit the style sheet.

We will begin by adding a border around our left menu.

In TopStyle, edit the border properties so that border-width is "thin", border-style is "solid", and border color is "silver".

⊟ border	thin solid silver
(border-width)	thin
(border-style)	solid
(color)	silver
⊞ border-bottom	
border-bottom-width	
⊞ border-color	
⊞ border-left	

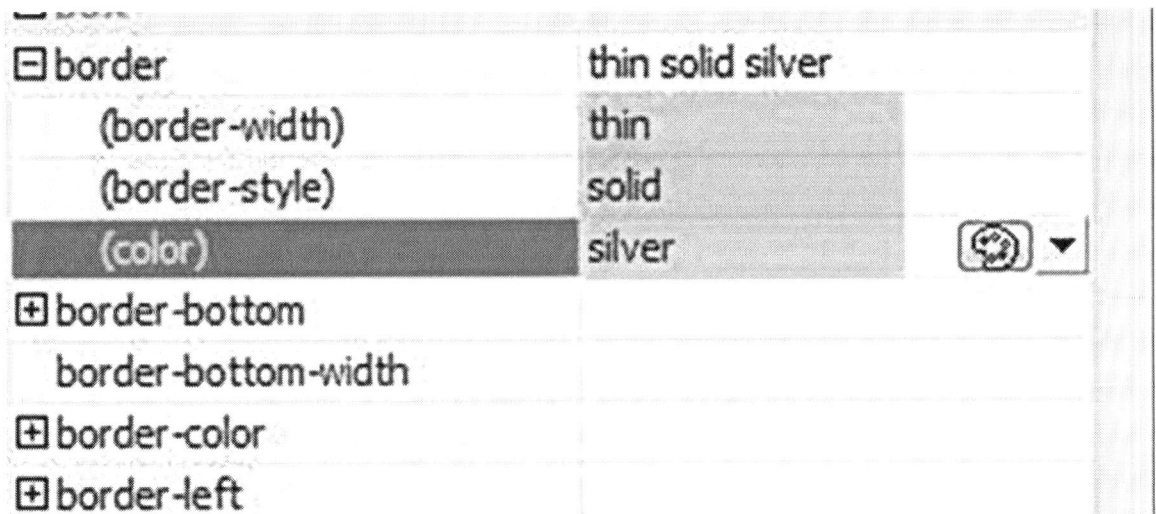

The style sheet will then look like this when you have finished:

#leftmenu { border: thin solid silver; }

Notice how the three properties are merged into a single line. This is something you will see a lot when defining properties.

(11.2.html and 11.2.css)

This is what the web page looks like so far:

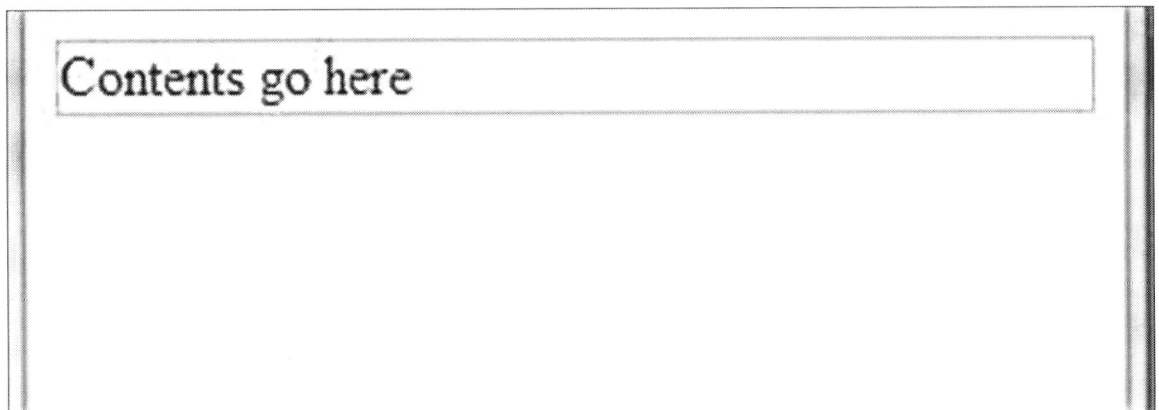

Contents go here

Note that the border is now around the content, but the content stretches horizontally across the top of the web page.

OK, let's now set the width of the box. In TopStyle, go to the **Box** category and set the width to 250 pixels:

#leftmenu { border: thin solid Silver; width: 250px; }

94

Now let's float the box on the left (again, the float property is in the **box** category):

#leftmenu { border: thin solid Silver; width: 250px; float: left; }

Here is the web page now:

```
Contents go here
```

(11.3.html and 11.3.css)

Now, let's take this one step further and create another box. This one we will use as the HEADER section of our web page.

In the style sheet, click on "New Selector" and choose "ID" on the "Advanced" tab. This time call it "header" and add it to your style sheet.

Create this ABOVE the leftmenu ID, so move it if necessary (you can copy, paste, and delete in the CSS editor just as you can with any word processor).

```
 1 #header {

   }

 5 #leftmenu {
        border: thin solid silver;
        width: 250;
        float: left;
   }
10


12
```

95

Add a thin, solid, silver border around it as we did with the previous example.

On the web page, add another div section that uses this new ID. Put it ABOVE the leftmenu section.

Here is how the web page looks now:

```
Contents go here
Contents go here
```

(11.4.html and 11.4.css)

OK, let us now make the header and leftmenu a little taller.

In the style sheet, add height = 150 pixels to the header, and height = 500 to the leftmenu (again, these properties are in the **box** category).

Here is the page now:

```
ID header




ID leftmenu
```

(11.5.html and 11.5.css)

Note: *this screenshot was taken from the preview window in TopStyle. It's a great way to see your layouts as you design them because it displays the ID names in the actual layout.*

That's starting to look a lot better.

OK, that's enough for now. We will continue with this in the next chapter.

12. A 2 Column Layout with Footer

In the last section we saw a simple two column layout.

I would like to create another two column layout, but this time with a footer area included in the design. I also want to give you "blank" templates for an HTML file and a CSS document. This is so you are not starting with nothing (daunting for CSS beginners), as you continue to learn how to create these layouts with confidence.

Let's create a blank html file:

<html>

<head>

<title></title>

<link rel="style sheet" media = "screen" type="text/css" href="styles.css">

</head>

<body>

</body>

</html>

(12.1.html)

Now, remind yourself of our initial layout plan:

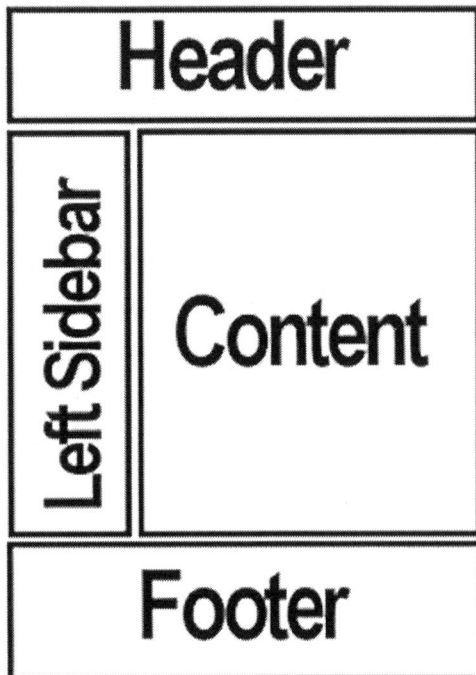

You can see four areas of the web page, namely, "header", "left sidebar", "content" and "footer". We now need to add the code to our template to define these areas. Here they are:

<div id="header">HEADER</div>

<div id="leftmenu">LEFT MENU</div>

<div id="content">CONTENT</div>

<div id="footer">FOOTER</div>

These divs need to go in the body section of the web page, so we end up with:

<html>

<head>

<title></title>

<link rel=<link rel="style sheet" href="styles.css" type="text/css">

</head>

<body>

<div id="header">HEADER</div>

<div id="leftmenu">LEFT MENU</div>

<div id="content">CONTENT</div>

<div id="footer">FOOTER</div>

</body>

</html>

(12.2.html)

OK, save that as "2columntemplate.html".

I have added some simple text into each of these divs, so that they will display in your HTML editor or web browser. This makes it easier to see how your layout is progressing.

Now we need to create a CSS file to hold our style information. We have already called it "styles.css" in the web page above, so make sure that when you saved it, you actually saved it as **styles.css**

In TopStyle, create a new CSS and make sure that you save it in the same folder as your template web page.

On the "Simple" tab, create selectors for "body", "h1", "h2", "h3", and "p".

Set the body to:

Font-family: Verdana, Geneva, Arial, Helvetica, sans-serif

Font-size: 1em

Set the H1 header to:

Font-size: 200%

Set the h2 header to:

Font-size: 160%

Set the h3 header to:

Font-size: 120%

Set p to:

Line-height: 120%

Create IDs for each of the four areas defined in the web page. These are: "header", "leftmenu", "content", and "footer" (without the quotes).

(12.2.css)

You can see what this page looks like so far without any properties defined in the style sheet:

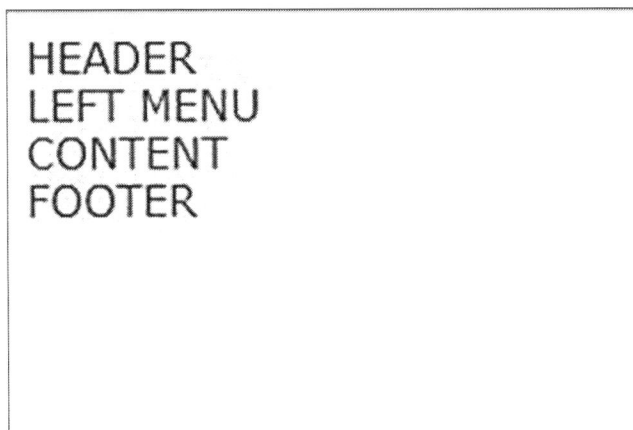

(12.2.css)

You can see what this page looks like so far without any properties defined in the style sheet:

HEADER
LEFT MENU
CONTENT
FOOTER

TopStyle's preview window actually gives us even more information on the formatting:

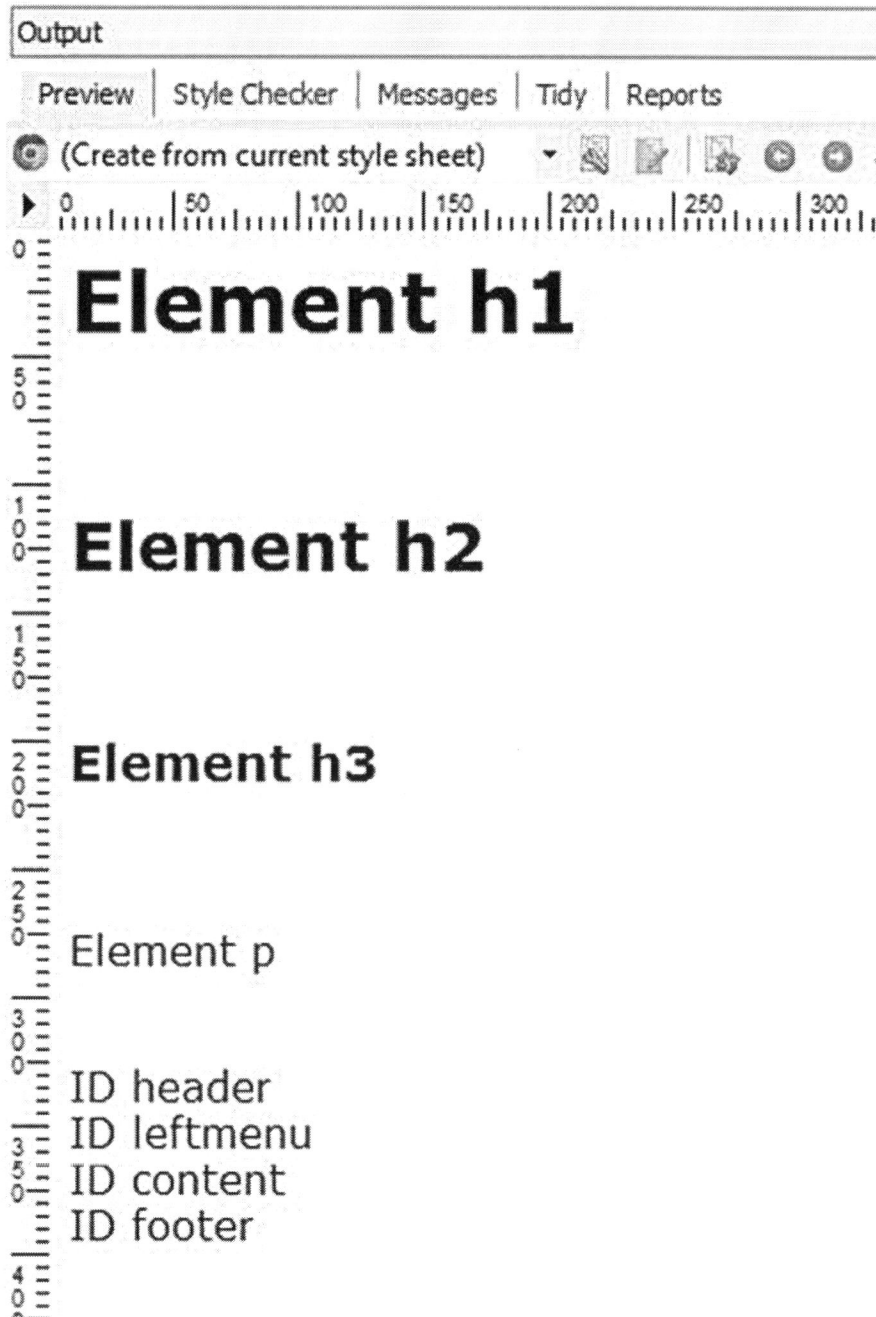

We are now ready to start adding the properties to each ID so that our webpage layout can be begin to take shape.

OK, so starting at the top, let's create the header area first.

In your CSS file, click between the curly brackets of the header ID. Add a 1px (1px length) solid border, with a color of your choice, and add a background color too. Do this in exactly same way as we did earlier in the book.

Just to help "pad" this out, add a padding of 5px to the top, left, bottom & right borders of the Header ID (padding is in the **box** category).

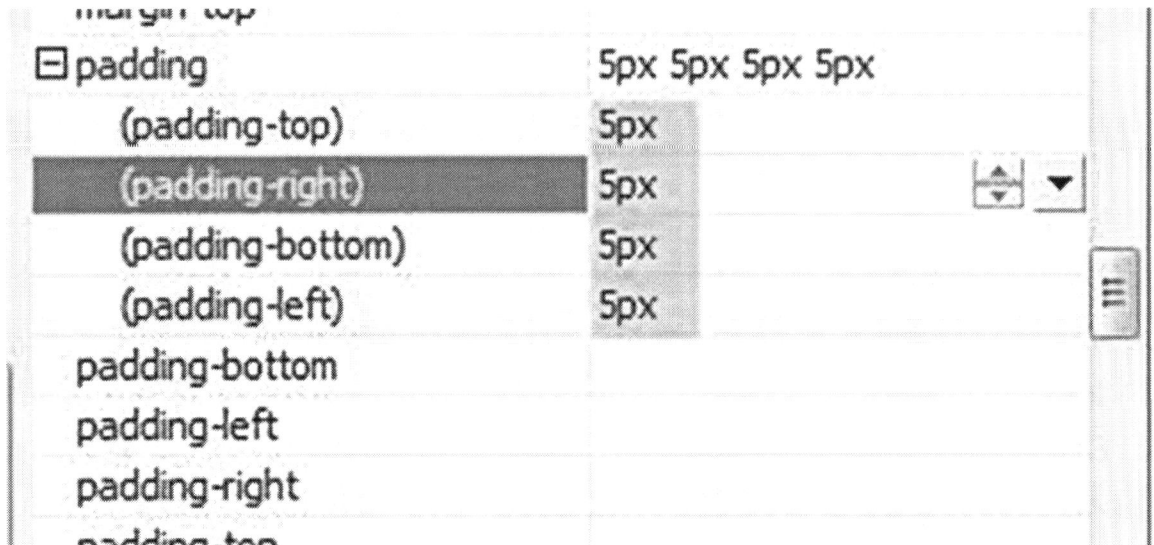

margin top	
⊟ padding	5px 5px 5px 5px
(padding-top)	5px
(padding-right)	5px
(padding-bottom)	5px
(padding-left)	5px
padding-bottom	
padding-left	
padding-right	
padding-top	

A Word About Padding

Padding can be defined for top, left, bottom & right separately. We want 5px padding on all sides, so set each to 5px. In the style sheet, the padding will have four values which are in this order: top, right, bottom, left (think clock face as a simple way to remember this sequence).

If all four paddings are the same value, so you can just use that single value in the padding properties, i.e., instead of:

padding: 5px 5px 5px 5px;

We could just write:

padding: 5px;

Other situations you may find when examining other people's CSS are when the padding value has two values, for example,

Padding: 5px 10px;

In this case, the first number represents the padding for the top and bottom. The second value represents the padding for the left and right.

You can also have three values in the padding.

Padding: 5px 10px 15px;

Here, the first number represents the padding for the top.

The second number represents the padding for the right and left.

And the third number represents the padding for the bottom.

OK, here is my style sheet so far, as seen in the TopStyle previewer:

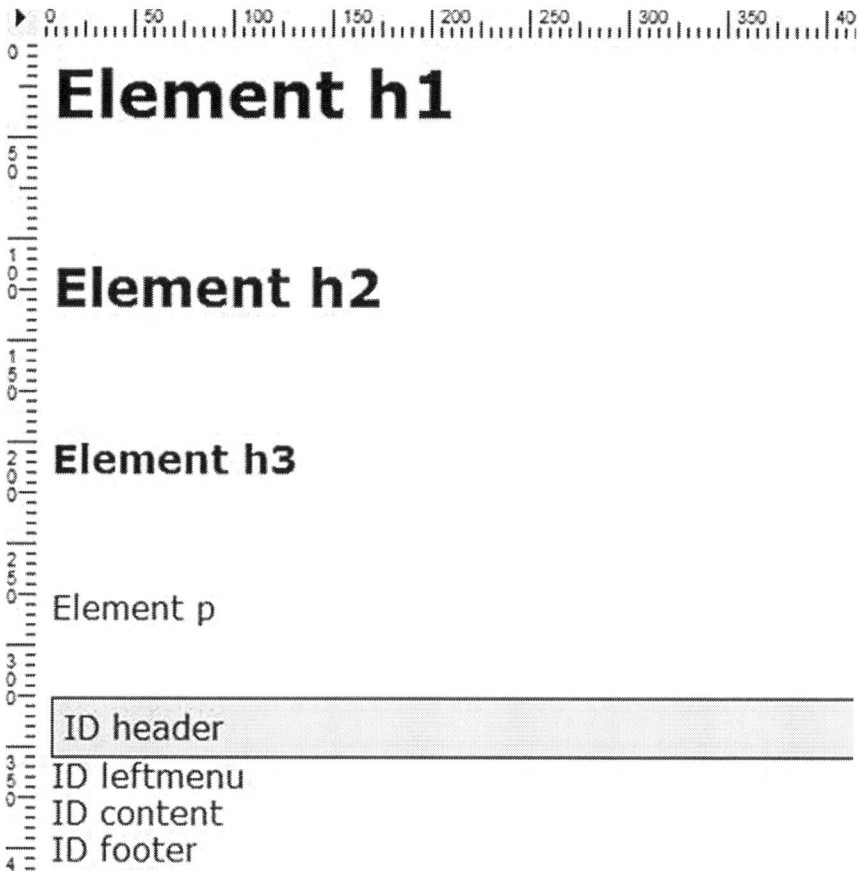

Element h1

Element h2

Element h3

Element p

ID header

ID leftmenu
ID content
ID footer

(12.3.css)

Copy and paste the styles from your header into each of the other three IDs in your style sheet.

Here is my layout so far:

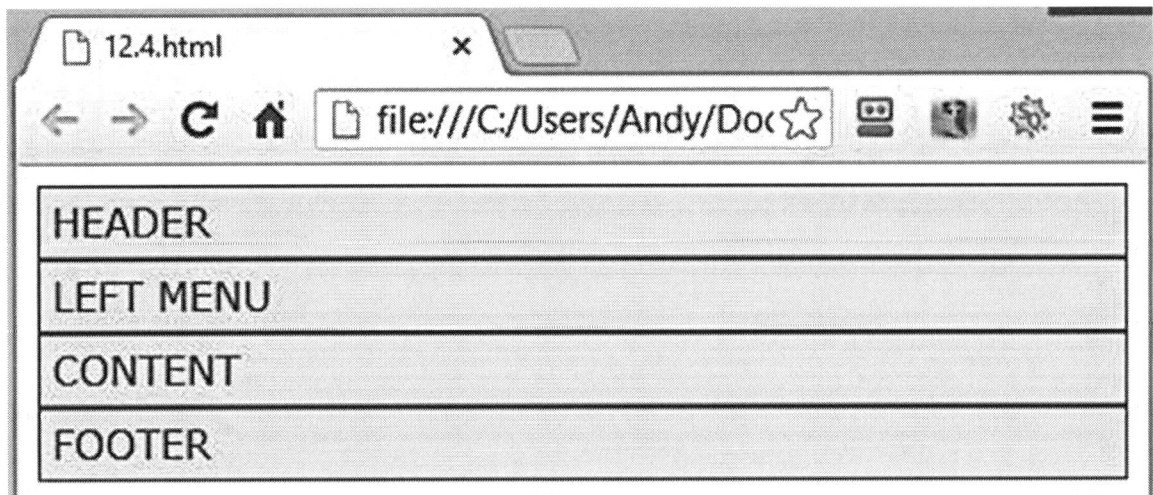

(12.4.html and 12.4.css)

Now, it's time to add some positioning elements.

Let's start by floating the left menu and giving it a fixed width. Add the float left style to your CSS file, for the leftmenu ID. Make it 250px wide.

I'll add a little text into the HTML document in the left menu and content areas. That will make it easier to see how the layout now looks.

Your layout should looks something like this:

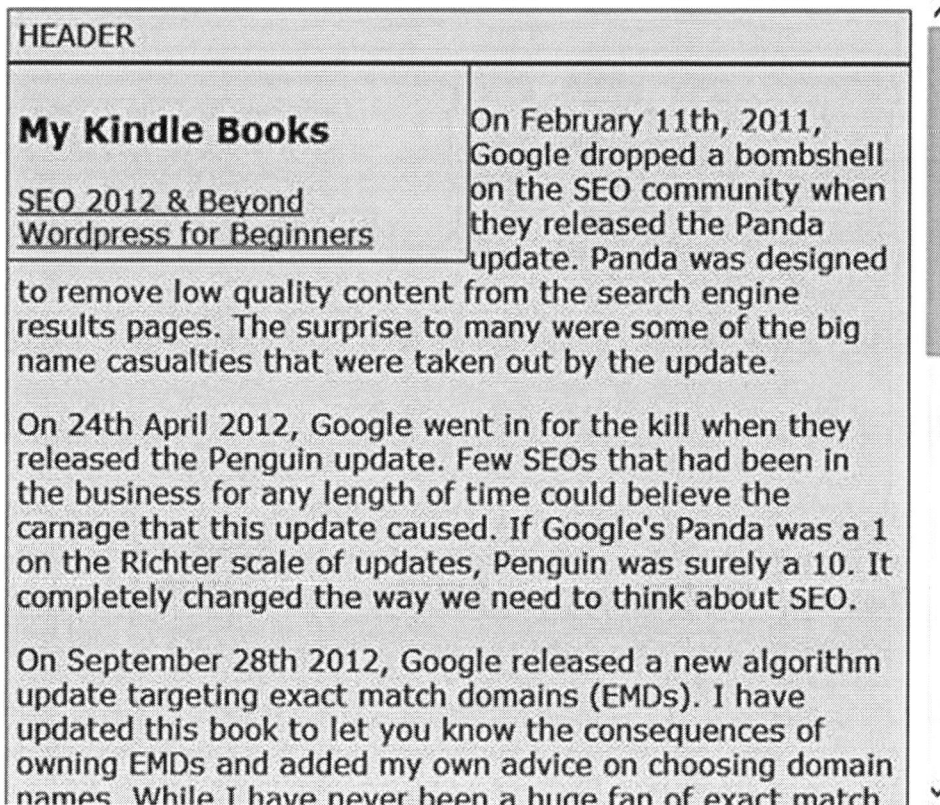

(12.5.html and 12.5.css)

That's starting to take shape nicely. However, do you notice the main content wrapping underneath the menu?

That means we don't really have a two column layout. What we actually have is a one column layout with a floated box (left menu). To define real columns, we need to assign vertical space to specific columns. If it were a true two column layout, then this wrapping would not happen.

So on that note, let's make is a 'true' two column layout.

To stop the main content wrapping into the menu column, we need to define a **left margin** for the content. The reason for this left margin is because we want to leave a certain amount of space on the left; space that the main content cannot cross, or use.

Enter a margin-left of 265px to the content ID.

Here is my web layout now:

(12.6.html and 12.6.css)

Now remove the color background from the main content area by deleting the color property from the Content ID.

Load the html file in your web browser and then try resizing it. See how the content column resizes to fit the screen?

Do you notice how the header and footer are touching the main content? Wouldn't it be nice if there was a little breathing space between these sections? Well, the margin property comes to our rescue yet again.

Define a bottom margin to the header, say 10px.

For the footer, define a margin-top of 10px.

(12.7.html and 12.7.css)

Question: What would happen if you added a 10px top & bottom margin to the content instead of the way we did it above? You can try it and see if you like, or just read the answer below.

Answer: The content is spaced nicely, but the menu remains attached to the header, as there is no margin between the header and left menu sections.

Before we finish for now, let's just check something. What happens if the menu is really long?

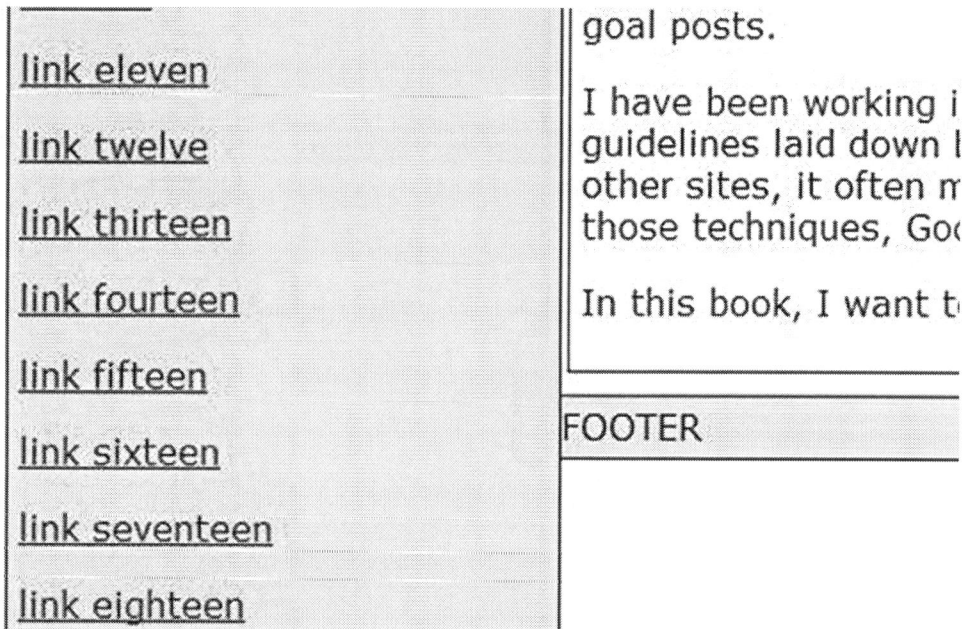

link eleven	goal posts.
link twelve	I have been working i
link thirteen	guidelines laid down l
	other sites, it often m
link fourteen	those techniques, Go(
link fifteen	In this book, I want t
link sixteen	FOOTER
link seventeen	
link eighteen	

(12.8.html and 12.8.css)

Whoops! The left part of the footer has been covered by the menu column. Fortunately, we can fix that with a simple property called "clear".

Clearing essentially reinstates the linear flow of the page, over-writing the floating menu. What that means in layman's terms is that the cleared element will appear underneath the last element on the page.

That is what we want - the footer appearing underneath the left menu.

Add the property "clear: both" to the footer ID. That will ensure the footer clears both columns.

(12.9.html and 12.9.css)

Congratulations! You have just built a true two-column CSS web layout.

Have a go at converting the left hand menu to a right hand menu. Remember, you only need to change two properties in your style sheet.

```
30 ⊟ #leftmenu {
         border: 1px solid navy;
         background-color: #dddfff;
         padding: 5px 5px 5px 5px;
         float: right;
35       width: 250px;
      └ }


   ⊟ #content {
         border: 1px solid navy;
40       padding: 5px 5px 5px 5px;
         margin-right: 265px;
         }
43
```

Here is what this basic page will then look like:

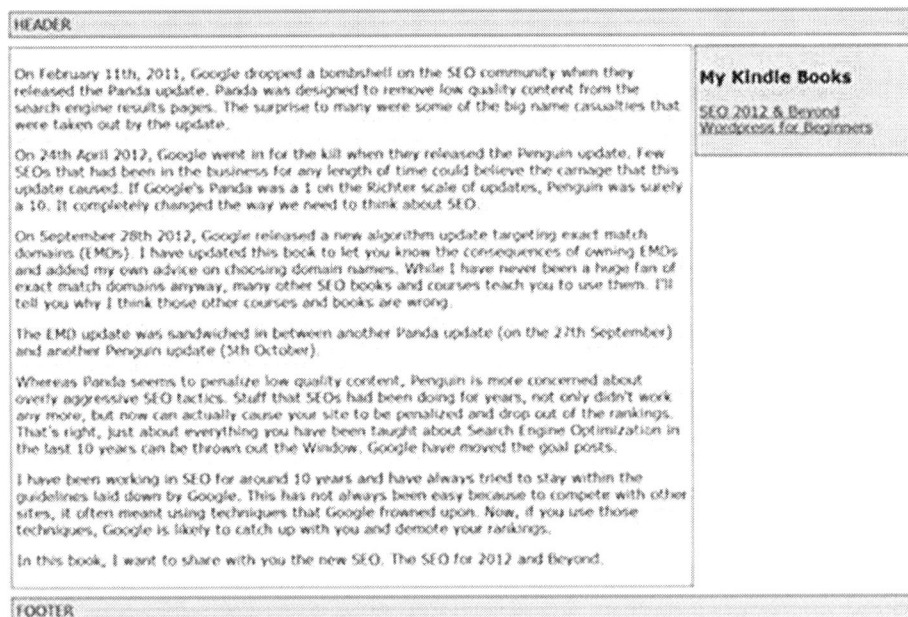

(12.10.html and 12.10.css)

In the next chapter, we will do a three-column layout, although the more adventurous of you can probably do that by now anyway.

13. A Simple Three Column Layout

In the last section you created a two column layout. Now I want to show you how easy it is to convert that into a three column layout.

As a reminder, here is the template we created in the last section:

(13.1.html and 13.1.css)

If you look at that layout, you can see that there are two changes we still need to make:

1. Create a right hand menu.
2. Adjust the width of the content section.

We will start off using the above HTML file and CSS. I suggest you open these files from the source code download, and save it as 3-col.html. Rename the style sheet as 3-col.css, and change the link in the HTML document to point to this new CSS file.

Let's now add the sections to the web page and style sheet first, and then we'll work on the properties.

In the HTML document, add the following code right after the section for the leftmenu:

<div id="rightmenu">RIGHT MENU HERE

</div>

Now, using TopStyle, add a new ID called rightmenu (from the "Advanced" tab).

Here is the new code that appears in the CSS:

#rightmenu {

}

In the CSS file, add a border like the one you have defined for your left menu.

Use the same padding as the left, and the same background-color too. Make the width 250px, again, the same as it is for the left menu, and then float the menu, but this time, float **RIGHT**.

NOTE: If you want to, you can copy the CSS properties for the left menu and paste it into the curly brackets of the rightmenu. Then you just need to change the properties.

If you view your template now, this is what it should look like:

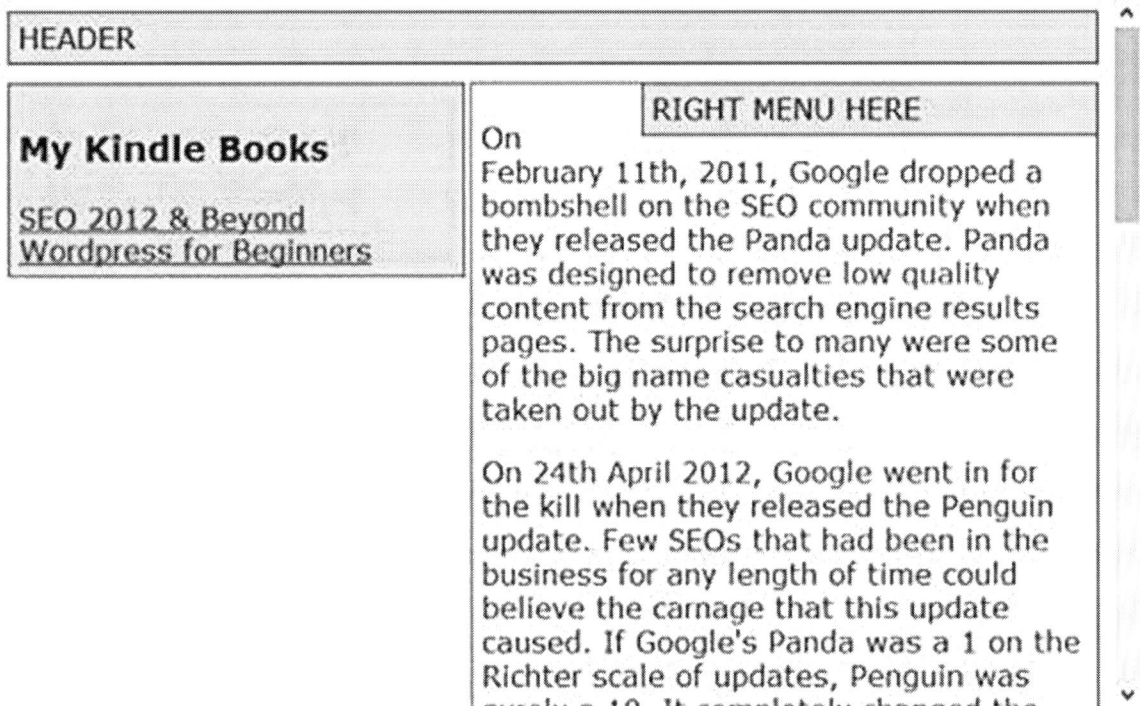

HEADER

My Kindle Books

SEO 2012 & Beyond
Wordpress for Beginners

RIGHT MENU HERE

On February 11th, 2011, Google dropped a bombshell on the SEO community when they released the Panda update. Panda was designed to remove low quality content from the search engine results pages. The surprise to many were some of the big name casualties that were taken out by the update.

On 24th April 2012, Google went in for the kill when they released the Penguin update. Few SEOs that had been in the business for any length of time could believe the carnage that this update caused. If Google's Panda was a 1 on the Richter scale of updates, Penguin was surely a 10. It completely changed the

(13.2.html and 13.2.css)

The content column is too wide as it runs under the right-hand menu.

We can fix that in the same way we did for the left menu - by adding a margin on the right of the content column. We will use the same margin width as we did for the left hand menu. Here is the code:

margin-right: 265px;

Add this code to the content ID in the style sheet.

Here is how the final page layout looks:

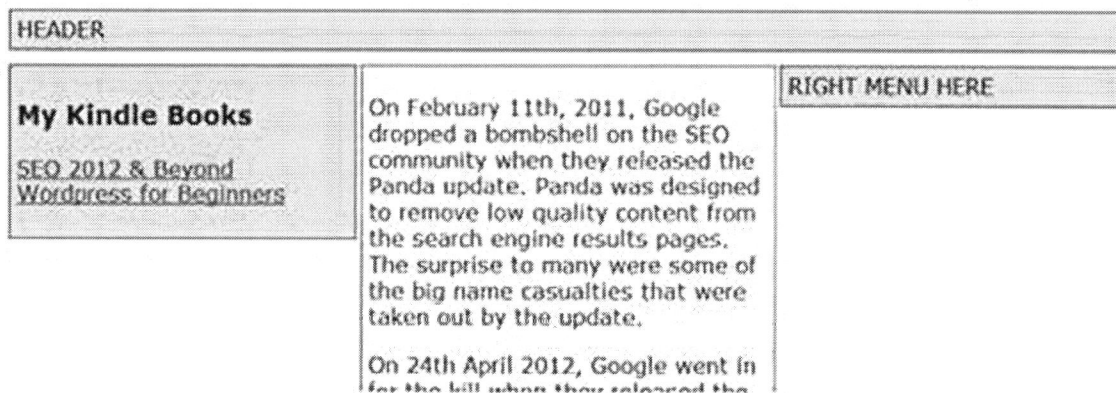

(13.3.html and 13.3.css)

This is a "floated: layout. What this basically means is that the menus are floated on the left and right sides.

The disadvantage of this type of layout is that the div sections in the html document must be in the correct order, or the layout won't work. You can see this if you change the order. In the example below, I have placed the right menu underneath the footer.

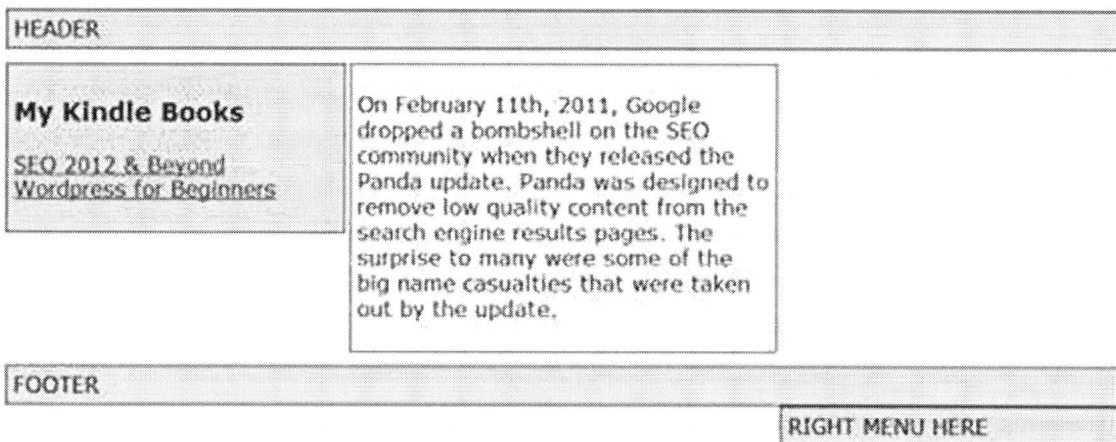

(13.4.html and 13.4.css)

In floated layouts, the sections are read in a linear fashion, and created in the order they appear in the HTML. When something is floated, it will be floated *after* the DIV that precedes it.

In the next section, we will start to look at positioned layouts. In these types of layouts, the order of the sections is not important. This is because we use CSS to define *exactly* where the sections are placed in the final HTML file.

14. The Box Model

In the last chapter we created a floated three-column CSS template.

Now I want us to start looking at positioned layouts, as these have the advantage for "divs" to be in any order in the HTML file (meaning the main content can be moved up the document to make it the first thing the search engines see when they spider your page).

These positioned layouts can be liquid (like the other templates we have built), or fixed width. We will cover both of these layouts in the remaining parts of this course.

Before we can start to create positioned layouts though, we do need to have a quick look at the "box model", as this is very important for the designer to know about when creating positioned layouts.

Basically, if you were a style sheet, you would view a web page as boxes of content. Everything is inside its own little box. Now, those boxes have dimensions, and some have borders, margins, and so on.

The box model is best represented as this diagram:

```
#box{
width: 300px;
Height: 200px;
padding: 10px;
margin: 10px;
border:1px solid #000
}
```

this is the content of the box,
this is the content of the box,
this is the content of the box,
this is the content of the box,
this is the content of the box,
this is the content of the box,
this is the content of the box,

(Content Area
of Box)
300px

10px
padding

10px
padding

1px
border

1px
border

10px
Margin

10px
Margin

Total Box Width:10+1+10+300+10+1+10 = 342
Total Box Height: 10+1+10+200+10+1+10 = 242;

NOTE: Margins are transparent, so the "visible" box is 322 x 222.

It should become immediately apparent why the box model is important to know. A 300px width box, isn't 300px wide! The box width is actually given by the sum of the left and right margins, border, and or padding, and the content width.

The height is given by the sum of the top and bottom margins, border, padding, and the content height.

What this all means, is that when designing CSS layouts, you must take into account padding, margins, and borders. The width you define in your style sheet is the width of the content of the box, BUT, you must add padding, margins, and borders to that.

If you have 300 pixels available to insert a box, you are better off working backwards. For example, if you want a 1 pixel border, a 5 pixel margin, and some padding of say 5 pixels, you would need to define your width as follows:

300 - (1x2) - (5x2) - (5x2), (this is width available minus two borders, and two paddings).

Your width declared in the style sheet will therefore be 278 pixels, and not 300! So with the border, margin, and padding mentioned above, this box will fill the 300 pixels available.

I understand that this is quite a bit to get your head around at this point, so we'll leave it there for now.

You can read up more on the box model if you want at:

http://www.w3.org/TR/REC-CSS2/box.html

15. Positioning Boxes Using Absolute Positioning

In the last chapter we looked at the box model, which is vital to creating CSS layouts. If you need reminding about the box model, then refer back to chapter 14, and go over it until you grasp the concept. Believe me, once you understand this, you will wonder what all the fuss was about.

I want to now look at the next part of this puzzle, which is how to position a box on the page using absolute positioning in CSS. This gives us absolute control over where our "boxes" are positioned on the web page, right down to 1 pixel accuracy.

In CSS it is possible to position a box (all items on a page are essentially contained in a box), anywhere on the page using absolute positioning.

Let's start off by creating a basic HTML template and a CSS file.

Here is my HTML document:

<html>

<head>

<meta http-equiv="Content-Type" content="text/html;

charset=iso-8859-1">

<title>Boxes</title>

<link rel="style sheet" media = "screen" type="text/css" href="boxes.css">

</head>

<body>

</body>

</html>

My CSS file is blank for now, but saved as **boxes.css**

(15.1.html and 15.1.css)

You can use these files yourself as we go through the examples in this chapter.

OK, so let's now create a box.

Add a new selector and go to the "Advanced" tab to select ID. Simply name your ID Box1.

Give the ID a width of 250px, height of 250px and a border as a thin black line. Note all of these properties are in the "**box**" category!

Here is the ID as defined in my style sheet:

#box1 { width: 250px; height: 250px; border: thin solid black; }

In our HTML File, we need to create a div for this box:

We can do that by simply adding this line to the body section of our HTML:

<div id="box1">BOX1</div>

Here is the page:

BOX1

(15.2.html and 15.2.css)

Now for the magic!

To position the box at a specific location, we add the following line to the ID declaration of our CSS file.

position: absolute;

NOTE: *the position property is not part of CSS Level1, so if you try to type this into your style sheet, TopStyle will give you an error message. To enable the position property, switch to using CSS Level 2 or higher.*

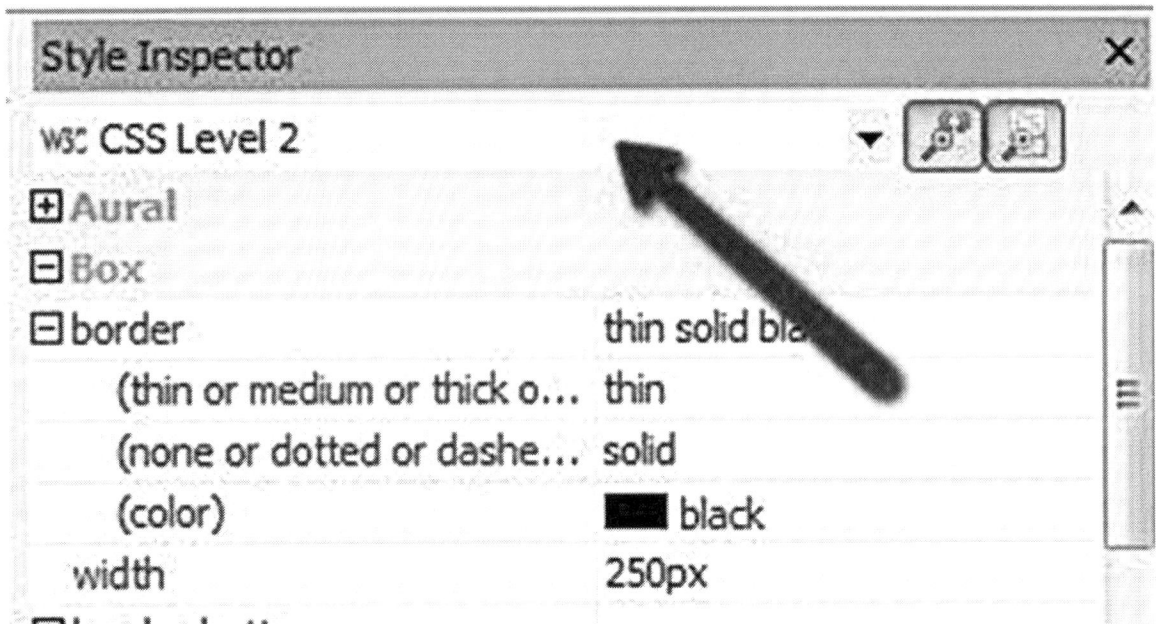

Adding the **position: absolute;** property to the CSS, is telling the web browser that we want to position this box somewhere on the page. We then need to tell the browser *exactly* where to place it. We do this by stating how far from the top, left, bottom, or right, we want the box to appear.

Let's add the position property first.

TopStyle does not include this property in the Style Inspector, so you will need to type it in manually. As you type the first part, you will get options:

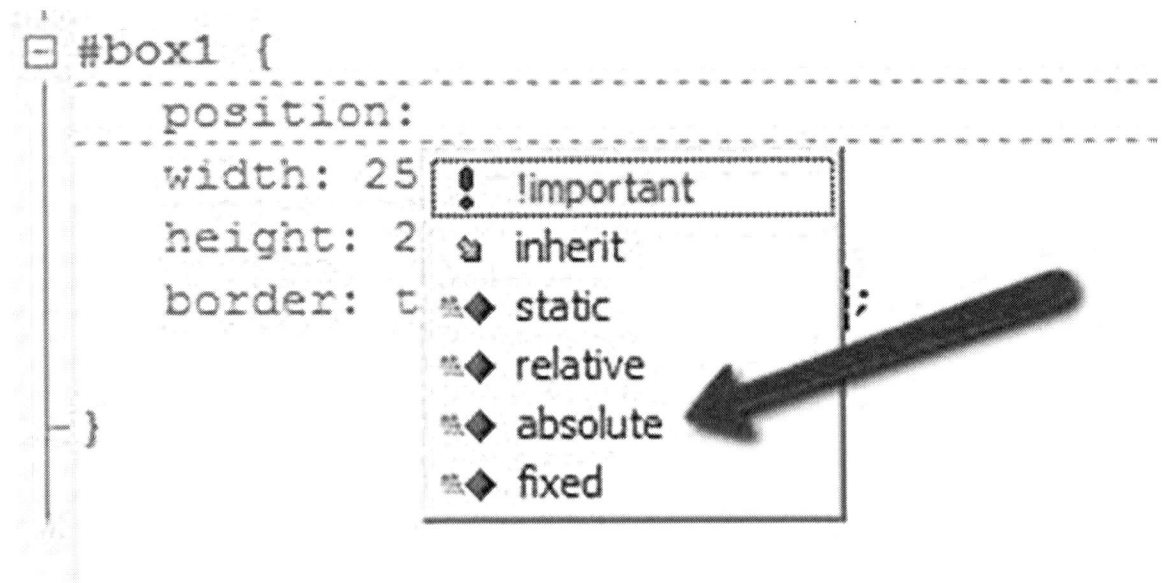

Just select absolute.

Now we need to type in the top and left coordinates of the box. Again, we need to type these into TopStyle manually, so add the following:

Top: 100px;
Left: 100px;

This will set the co-ordinates of the box at 100 pixels from the top and 100 pixels from the left:

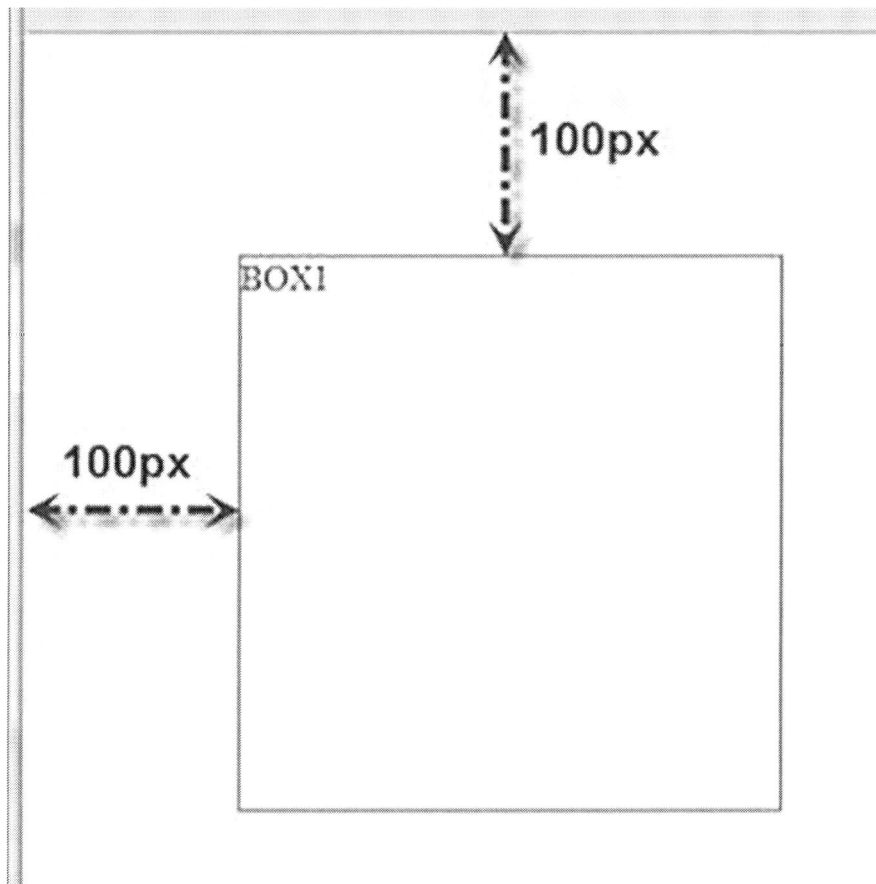

(15.3.html and 15.3.css)

Here's how the CSS is looking thus far:

```
#box1 {
position:absolute;
top: 100px;
left: 100px;
width: 250px;
height: 250px;
border: thin solid black;   }
```

What the absolute positioning elements actually do is to completely remove the box from the flow of the document. You can see this if we add some text to the page:

On February 11th, 2011, Google dropped a bombshell on the SEO community when they released the Panda update. Panda was designed to remove low quality content from the search engine results pages. The surprise to many were some of the big name casualties that were taken out by the update.

On 24th April 2012, Google went in for the kill when they released the Penguin update. Few SEOs that had been in the business for any length of time could believe the carnage that this update caused. If Google's Panda was a 1 on the Richter scale of updates, Penguin was surely a 10. It completely changed the way we need to think about SEO.

On September 28th 2012, Google released a new algorithm update targeting exact match domains (EMDs). I have updated this book to let you know the consequences of owning EMDs and added my own advice on choosing domain names. While I have never been a huge fan of exact match domains anyway, many other SEO books and courses teach you to use them. I'll tell you why I think those other courses and books are wrong.

(15.4.html and 15.4.css)

So what happens if we add another box that happens to be placed over some of the same space on the web page? The best way to illustrate this is to have a look, so here is my second box:

```
#box2{
position: absolute;
top: 150px;
left: 150px;
width: 50px;
height:50px;
border: thin solid Black;
}
```

Note that this one is positioned inside the first box:

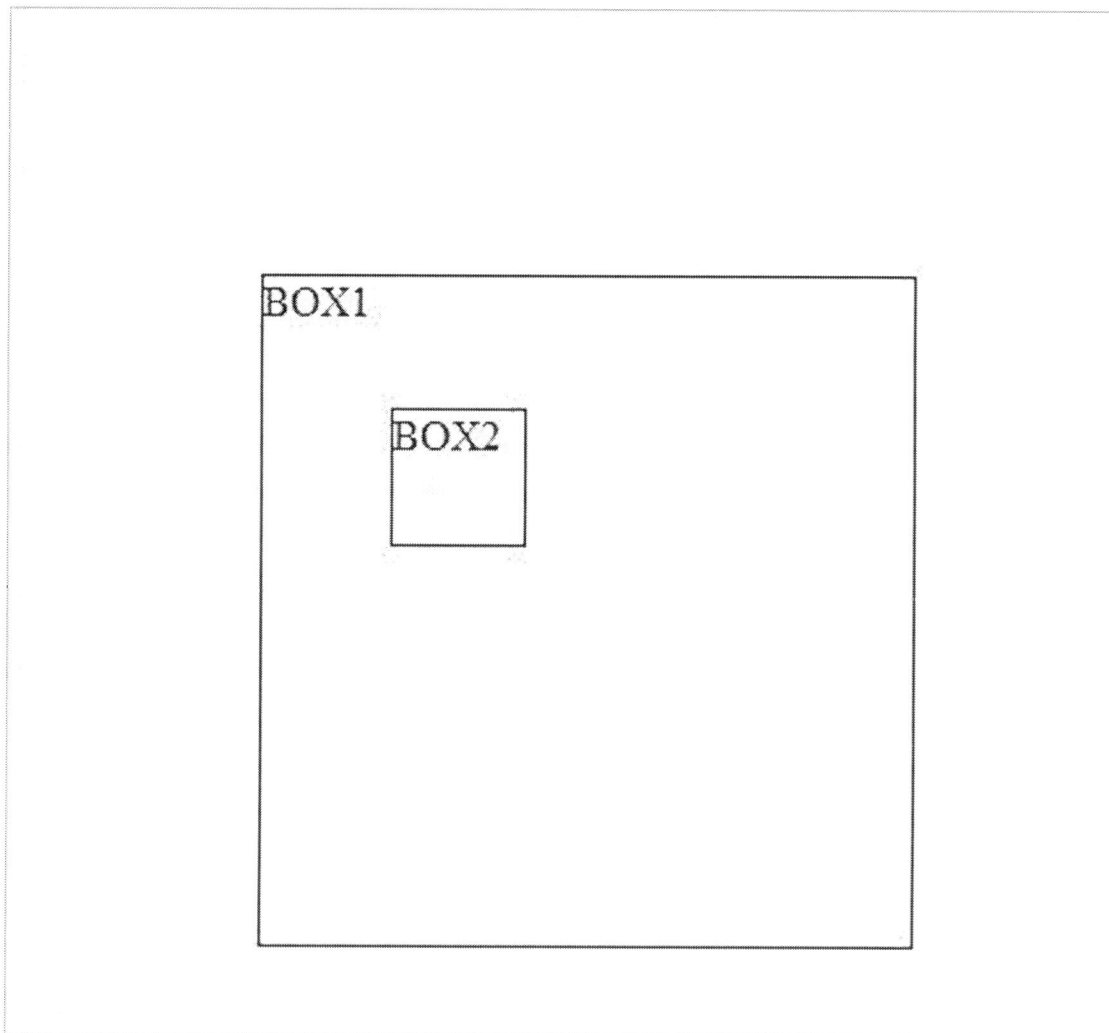

The HTML for this is simple:

<div id="box1">BOX1</div>

<div id="box2">BOX2</div>

(15.5.html and 15.5.css)

Both of these boxes are positioned relative to the top left corner of the screen. However, the position of a box is not always relative to the top left of the screen.

It is also possible to position a box relative to another box.

We use this HTML as an example:

<div id="box1">BOX1

<div id="box2">BOX2</div>

</div>

Can you see what have we done here?

We have placed the second box INSIDE the div tags of the first box.

Now, when the browser looks to position the second box, it does not take its calculation from the top left of the screen, but the top left of the parent box, in this case, that's box 1.

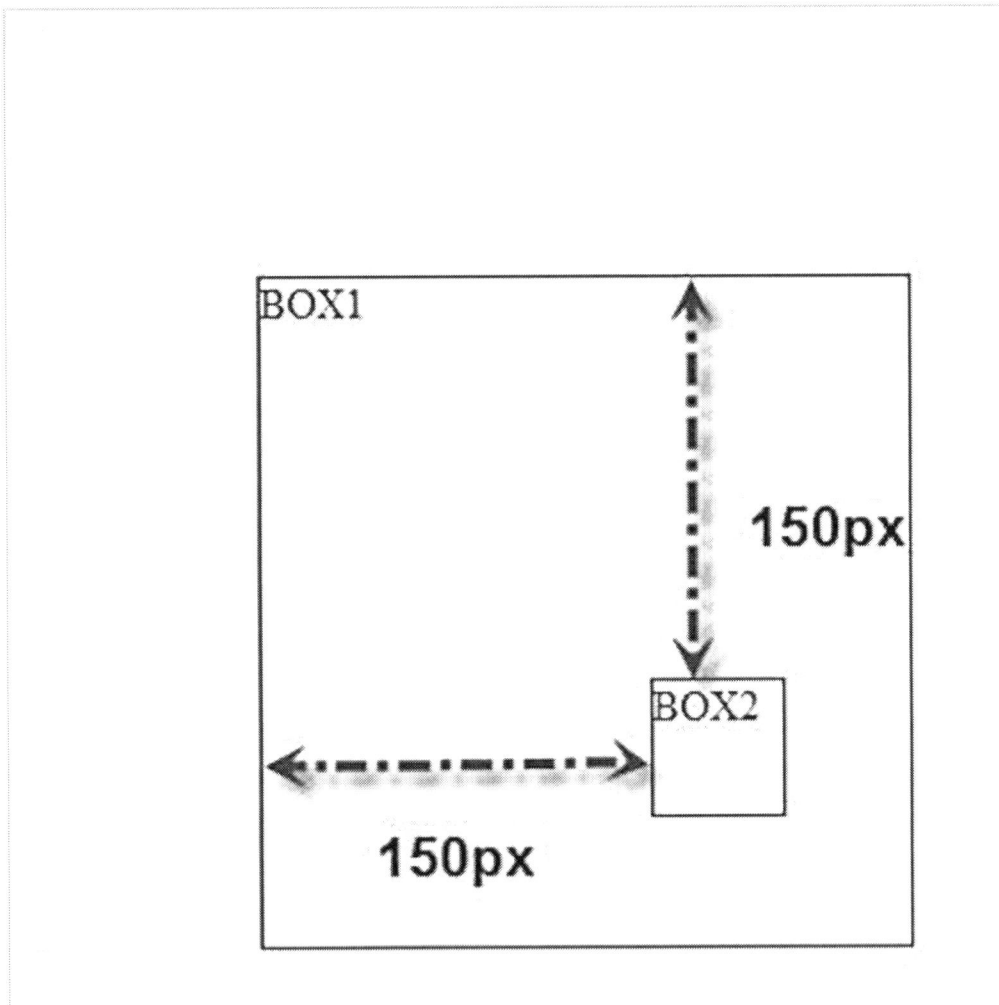

That means the second box will appear 150px down, and 150px from the left of the top left corner of box 1.

(15.6.html and 15.6.css)

When you use absolute positioning, it is important to remember that the position is calculated using the "parent element", and not necessarily from the sides of the browser screen. So if you include a box inside another box, the outer box becomes the parent.

We will leave this for now, but do have a play around to get some practice.

So far, we have positioned the boxes using top and left. However, you can also use bottom and right. Try using bottom and right to position your boxes. How about using some other unit instead of pixels for positioning?

If you want to read more about CSS positioning, here is an excellent article:

http://www.w3schools.com/css/css_positioning.asp

16. The Two Column Positioned Layout

In the last chapter we looked at absolute positioning of boxes on the screen. You learned that the coordinates which are defined as "absolute" are not always taken from the upper left hand corner of the screen. You should go back and read chapter 15 if you are not yet comfortable with this, as it's a very important aspect of CSS.

Now I want to build on what we have done so far. Remember, we are looking to produce a "positioned" three-column layout template that you can use and modify for your own sites. Now we will produce a positioned two-column layout (in baby steps of course).

Let's start with our basic templates:

Here's the HTML file:

```
<html>
<head>
<title></title>
<link rel="style sheet" media = "screen" type="text/css" href="styles.css">
</head>
<body>
<div id="header">HEADER</div>
<div id="content">CONTENT</div>
<div id="rightmenu">RIGHT MENU</div>
<div id="footer">FOOTER</div>
</body>
</html>
```

And here's the CSS:

```
body { font-family: Verdana, Geneva, Arial, Helvetica, sans-serif;
       font-size: 70%; }
#header {}
#rightmenu {}
#content {}
#footer {}
```

(16.1.html and 16.1.css)

Add borders to each of the main sections of the page so you that can see what is happening.

Here is the border I'm adding:

border: thin solid black;

(16.2.html and 16.2.css)

There's nothing positioned yet, so let's do that by starting with the header.

Add the following two lines to define the height and margin of the header:

height: 90px;

margin: 0px 0px 10px 0px;

NOTE: *The margin above has four numbers. This is a shorter way of creating a margin declaration (rather than having separate entries for margin-top, margin-left, etc.).*

The four numbers you see in the example above refer to the four margins available, starting with the top margin, and working in a clock-wise direction, right, bottom, and then left.

So our margin declaration above has a margin of 10px for the **bottom**, and top, left, and right margins, are set at 0px.

Remember that other shortcut we mentioned earlier?

If you want the same margin for all four positions, you can just combine them all into one declaration, i.e., margin: 10px;

Now, we want to add a margin on the right of the main content area to reserve a place for the right menu. We can do this by adding the following code to the content ID:

margin-right: 30%;

Setting this using a percentage means the right margin will always be 30% of the total width of the screen, instead of a fixed width like we saw earlier.

We'll also add some padding:

padding: 10px;

We don't need to position the main content ID using absolute positioning because it will naturally flow on from the header. However, the right menu will need absolute positioning so that it will be positioned outside the normal flow of the document.

```
┌────────────────────────────────────────────────────┐
│HEADER                                                │
│                                                      │
│                                                      │
│                                                      │
│                                                      │
│                                                      │
└────────────────────────────────────────────────────┘
┌───────────────────────────────────┐
│ CONTENT                            │
│                                    │
├────────────────────────────────────────────────────┐
│RIGHT MENU                                            │
├────────────────────────────────────────────────────┤
│FOOTER                                                │
└────────────────────────────────────────────────────┘
```

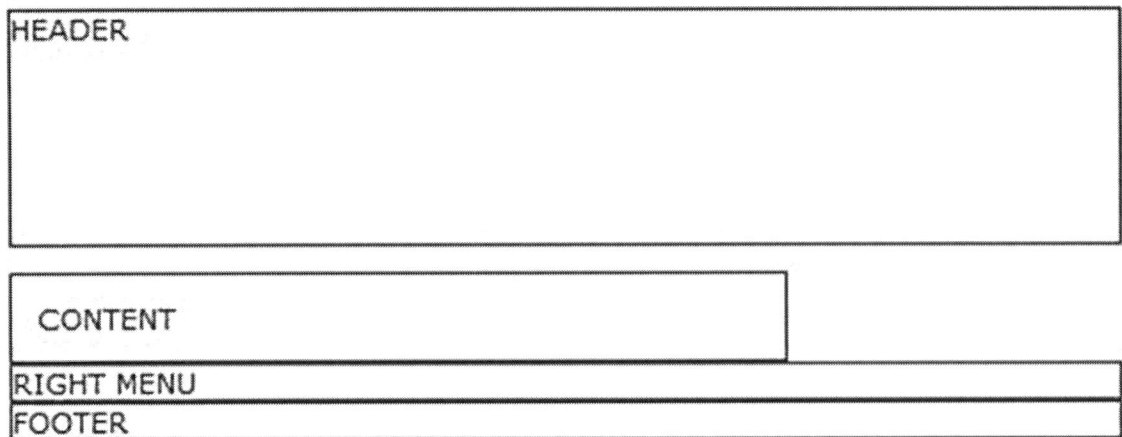

(16.3.html AND 16.3.css)

Looking at the template, you will see the space reserved for the right menu. However, you will also have realized that there is nothing new so far.

OK, so let us now position the right menu:

position: absolute;

Now, we want to position it below the header which is 90px high, plus margin (don't forget the box model). Add this line of code:

top: 110px;

This will place the menu 115 pixels from the top of the screen. We also want to place it on the right of the screen, so we need to set the "right" property:

right: 10px;

This places our menu 10 pixels from the right.

We need to also set the width of the menu. We gave ourselves a right margin on the content are of 30%, so let's try a 25 % width for our menu:

width: 25%;

And finally, let's add some padding:

padding:10px;

Here is how our template looks now, with the right menu positioned using absolute positioning:

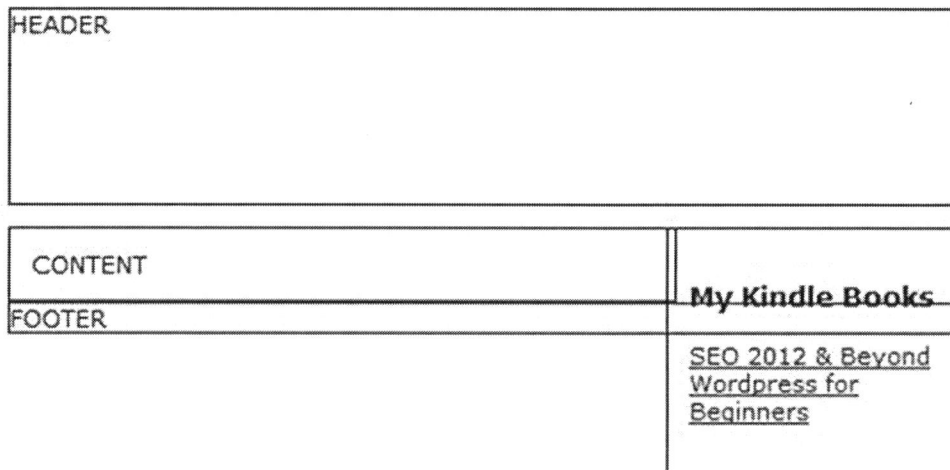

HEADER

CONTENT

FOOTER

My Kindle Books

SEO 2012 & Beyond
Wordpress for
Beginners

(16.4.html and 16.4.css)

You will notice that I have added some text to the right menu. Oh dear! Everything was looking so good up until now! What has happened to the footer?

This is a common problem with the footer menu in CSS positioned templates, but it's a problem that can be easily overcome once you know how. The easiest solution is to set the right hand margin of the footer so that this overlap doesn't happen. This is as simple as adding the following line to the footer ID in the CSS file:

margin-right: 30%;

I will also add a margin-top of 5px, just so that the footer is separated slightly from the content box.

Here is the resulting template (starting to look a lot better now!):

HEADER

CONTENT

FOOTER

My Kindle Books

SEO 2012 & Beyond
Wordpress for Beginners

(16.5.html and 16.5.css)

In the next chapter, we will continue with this. However, there is some experimenting you can do before then.

Try to change the style sheet so that the menu appears on the left, not the right. The more you play around with these things, the quicker you will learn.

17. Column Positioned Layout

In the last chapter we built a positioned two column layout. Now we will take it one step further, and turn the template into a three column layout.

Here is the two column template we created in the last session:

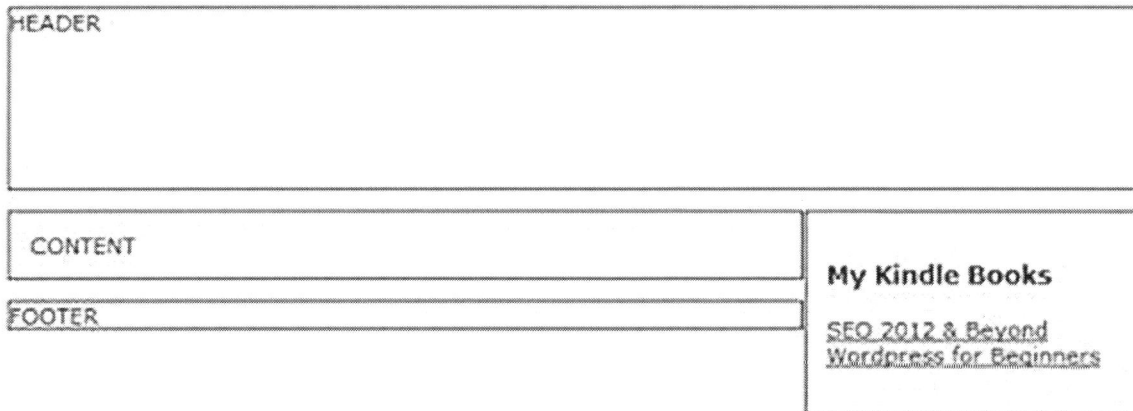

```
HEADER




```
```
CONTENT
                                              My Kindle Books
FOOTER
                                              SEO 2012 & Beyond
                                              Wordpress for Beginners
```

To make this a three column layout, we need to adjust both the content and header so that there's room to insert a left menu. We also need to define a new ID to hold the left menu information.

Let's start by adding the necessary code to the HTML document. You can add it anywhere in the HTML body, since we are positioning it using the absolute property. Here is the code:

<div id="leftmenu">LEFT MENU</div>

NOTE: I have called the ID "leftmenu", so make sure you type it exactly the same in the style sheet. Also note that it is not always a good idea to call your menus left or right; since using CSS, you can quickly swap them around. "menu1" and "menu2" might be a better choice of name. We will look at swapping the menus later in this chapter.

OK, now we need to change the style sheet.

Firstly, add a new ID called "leftmenu".

What I am going to do here is copy the properties from the right menu code:

```
#rightmenu { border: thin solid black;
position: absolute;
top: 115px;
right: 10px;
width: 25%;
padding: 10px;
}
```

Next I paste this code into the curly property brackets of the leftmenu ID. We can then simply modify only the bits that need changing.

So in this case, we need to position it from the left side of the screen, not the right as in the above code. Therefore change right: 10px, to left: 10px.

Here is my modified code:

```
#leftmenu {
border: thin solid black;
position: absolute;
top: 115px;
left: 10px;
width: 25%;
padding: 10px;
}
```

Here is how the new template looks so far:

You will see that the left menu is now in position, but it overlaps the main content and footer boxes, so let's fix this.

In the content ID, you already have a line that says:

margin-right: 30%;

This leaves a 30% margin on the right of the screen to accommodate the right menu. We need to do the same again, only this time, it's for the left side, i.e., add a left margin:

margin-left: 30%;

Here is how the template looks now:

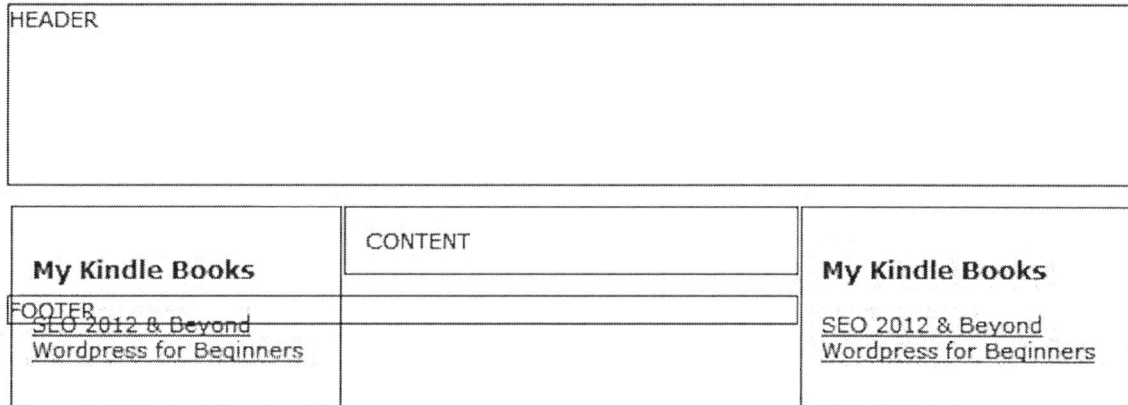

(17.2.html and 17.2.css)

OK, the only problem remaining is the footer. It overlaps the vertical space assigned for the menu, so we need to add the same left margin to the footer ID in order to correct the page layout.

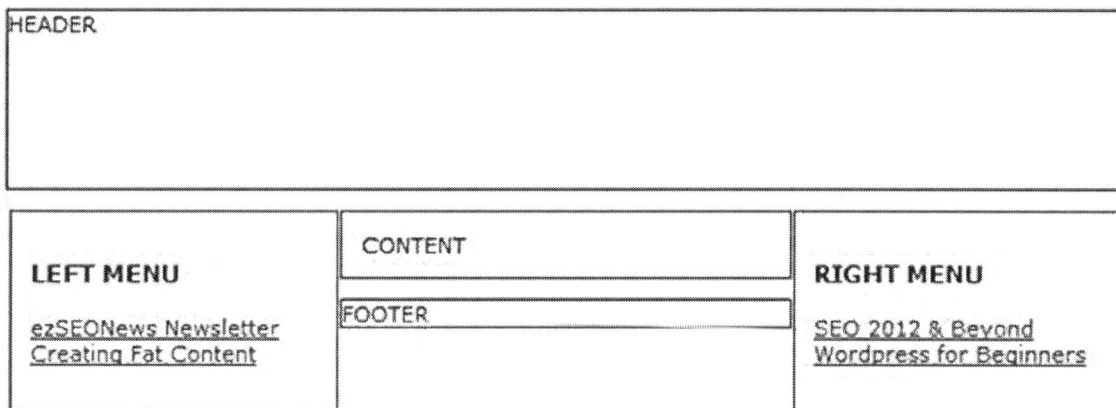

(17.3.html and 17.3.css)

OK, finally in this chapter, I promised to show you how easy it was to swap menus around, so let's do that now.

We're going to move the left menu to the right, and the right menu to the left. To do this, we only need to edit the CSS.

In the CSS file, locate the leftmenu ID, and change:

left: 10px;

to

right: 10px;

Now locate the rightmenu ID, and change:

right: 10px;

to

left: 10px;

That's it! Here is how our template looks now:

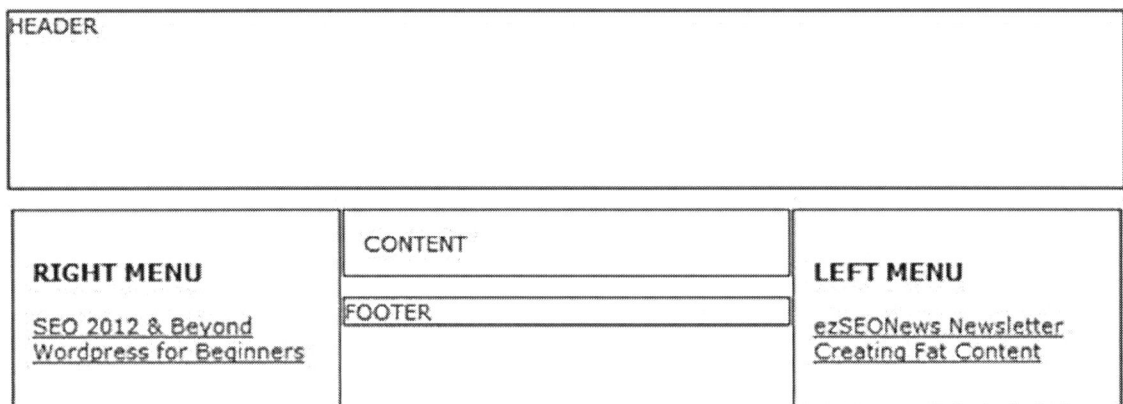

(17.4.html and 17.4.css)

See how easy that was? The left menu is now on the right, and vice versa.

This is one of the reasons CSS is so useful. You can make sweeping changes to the format and layout of your entire site, simply by modifying bits of code in a single CSS file.

You now have a perfectly acceptable three-column layout which you can modify and use for your own sites. However, the next few chapters will look at ways to spice up these templates.

18. Creating a Basic Menu Using CSS

With the basis of our three-column template established, the last remaining piece of the jigsaw is the navigation system.

When most people start building websites, their navigation menu is usually created with a table, using either plain text links, or graphic buttons.

From an SEO point of view, text links are far better. This is because the anchor text is used by the search engines to help determine what a page is about. It would be a shame if after creating a CSS layout we then had to resort to using a table for navigation. Fortunately though, we don't. We can create pure CSS navigation systems.

18.1. Creating a Menu from an Unordered List

A menu is just a list of links. HTML gives us tags for quickly creating lists, so that is a great option for our CSS based navigations system, i.e., lists modified using CSS.

Ordered lists are created in HTML with the following code:

```
<ol>
<li>Item 1</li>
<li>Item 2</li>
<li>Item 3</li>
</ol>
```

These lists have numbers preceding each item in them. We generally don't want to use numbers in our menus.

Unordered lists don't have these numbers, but do have bullets preceding each item.

Unordered lists are created in HTML with the following code:

```
<ul>
<li>Item 1</li>
<li>Item 2</li>
<li>Item 3</li>
</ul>
```

Here are visual examples of how both "ordered" and "unordered" lists appear:

Ordered List:

1. one
2. two
3. three
4. four

Unordered List:

* one
* two
* three
* four

(18.1.html)

Have a look at the source code behind the page.

The unordered list is the one we will use in the tutorial for creating our menus. Don't worry about the bullet marks because with CSS we can remove them quickly and easily.

Here is an example of a simple menu built with an unordered list, and CSS:

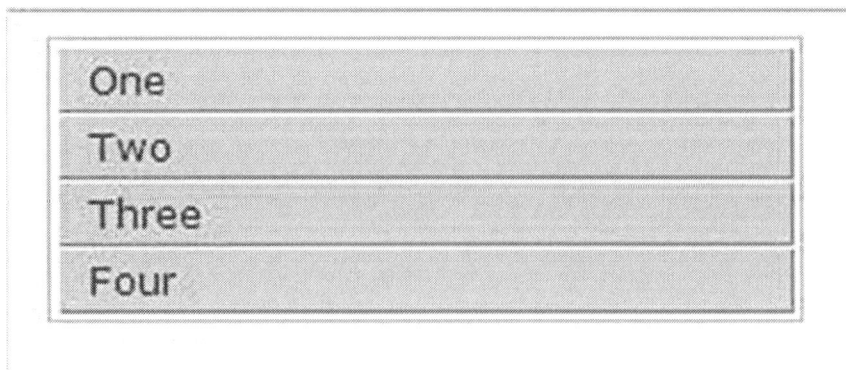

One

Two

Three

Four

Let's now look at how you can do this for yourself.

Create a new HTML file, and a blank CSS file.

(18.2.html and 18.2.css)

Link the CSS file to the HTML document. After the opening <body> tag in the HTML file, type in the code for an unordered list, and include a few items.

Here is the list code I am using for my example:

```
<ul>
  <li>one</li>
  <li>two</li>
  <li>three</li>
  <li>four</li>
</ul>
```

What we have done is create a list of four items. Each item will eventually be a text link pointing to a web page.

OK, here is my page so far:

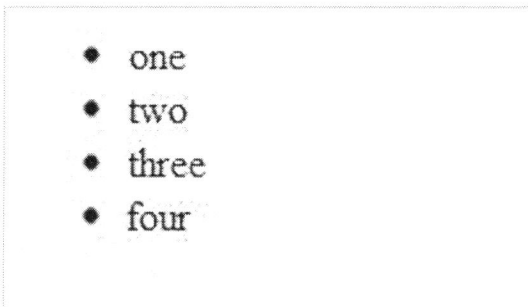

- one
- two
- three
- four

(18.2.html and 18.2.css)

Nothing special as yet, because all we have is a normal unordered list.

Let's now add an ID to our style sheet to handle the main menu.

```
#mainmenu {
}
```

OK, so we have an ID to use for the main menu (an ID is suitable for this as we will only use the main menu once per page).

Now, in this ID, let's define the main features of the menu, i.e., the width and the preferred font.

Here is mine:

```
#mainmenu {
        width: 250px;
        font-family: Verdana, Geneva, Arial, Helvetica, sans-serif;
}
```

This ID has a width of 250px, and a font-family.

If you check the web page, it still shows an unordered list. That is because the menu has not been assigned an ID. We need to add that to the HTML file. In order to assign the menu to the mainmenu ID, we need to first surround the menu code with <div></div> tags.

We can then insert the ID into the opening <div> like this:

```
<div id="mainmenu">
<ul>
 <li>one</li>
 <li>two</li>
 <li>three</li>
 <li>four</li>
</ul>
</div>
```

As soon as you save your two documents, you can see the change in font and capitalization. The width isn't apparent, as there is no border around the menu yet, so let's add a border:

border: thin dashed Silver;

Now our menu is starting to take shape:

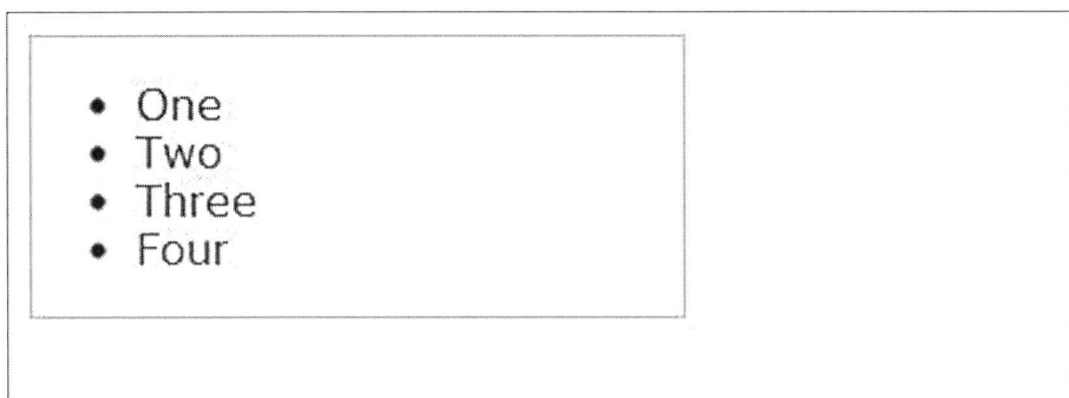

(18.3.html and 18.3.css)

However, there are still those bullet marks that we need to remove, plus an unordered list has an "indent" to leave room for the bullet mark. So we need to remove the bullet and also the indent. To do this, we have to modify how unordered lists are displayed.

However, we don't want to remove any bullets from a list that we might include in the main page content, so we need to tie this bullet removal to the lists inside the "mainmenu" ID only. Here is how we do that. First add the following code to your style sheet:

```
#mainmenu ul {
}
```

This means that whenever a <ul> tag is found inside a main menu, it will be modified according to the properties in the curly brackets.

To remove the bullets, we set the "list-style" of the ID:

```
list-style: none;
```

NOTE: *There are a variety of list styles you can use in your CSS templates. Some are more useful for lists appearing in the main content of your pages rather than the menus, so I'll leave you to experiment with those.*

OK, here is what my menu looks like now:

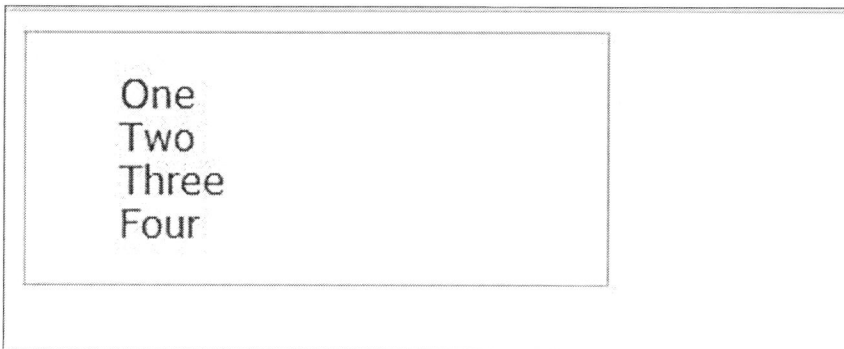

(18.4.html and 18.4.css)

Great, we have removed the bullets and have the beginnings of a real menu, but what about the indent?

The indents are due to the browsers' default style sheets. They add a margin and padding to the list items. However, as you know a browsers' default settings can be over-ridden. Here we will set the margin and padding to zero:

```
Margin: 0px;
```

```
Padding: 0px;
```

137

This will set the margin and padding of unordered lists (in the mainmenu ID).

Now, for this to be a real menu it needs to have links. So let's create a few so we can see how the menu will look.

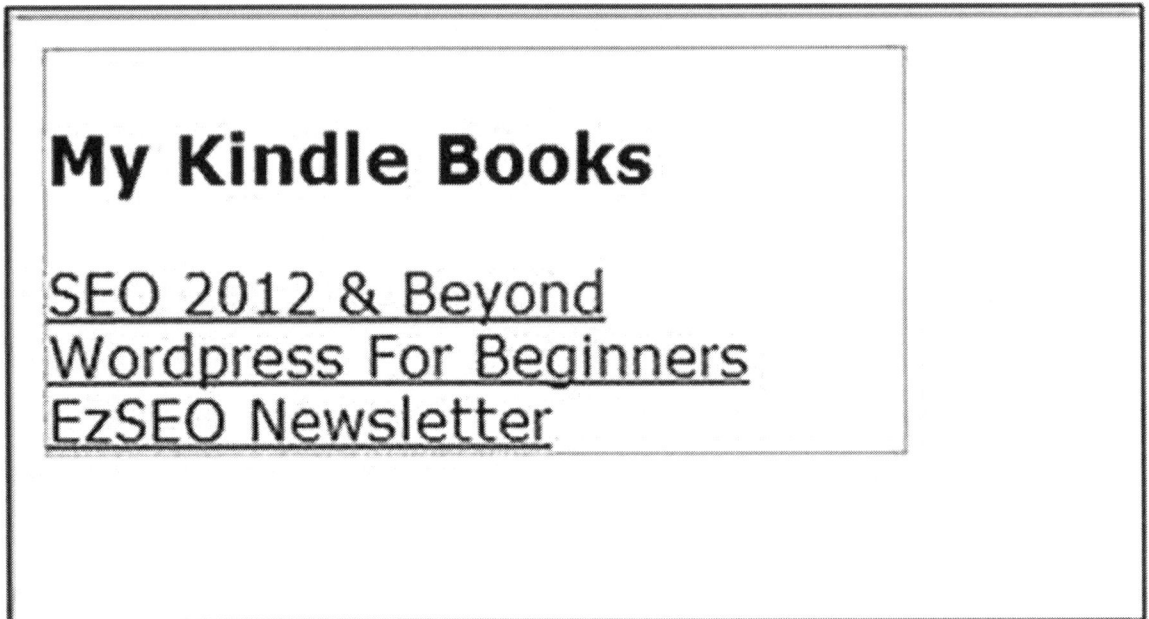

NOTE: *Just insert the HTML code for a link between each <li></li> tag.*

(18.5.html and 18.5.css)

Notice how the links are right up against the left and bottom borders of the box. How would you add a little white space around these edges? Have a go and see if you can get it right.

OK, so we now have a perfectly adequate menu, but it's far from being impressive or eye-catching.

In the next chapter, we will look at how to improve on this basic menu style.

19. Menu Eye Candy

Here is the basic menu we created in the previous chapter:

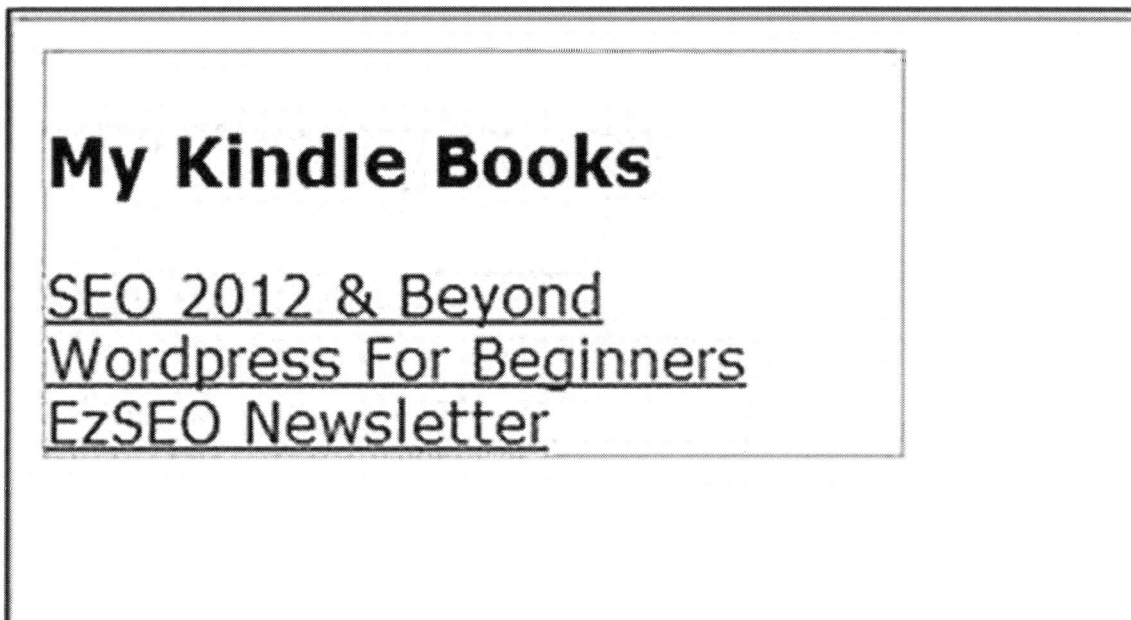

(18.5.html and 18.5.css)

Let's work on this to make it look much more pleasing on the eye.

Firstly, how about removing the underlines from the menu links?

We don't want to do this for all links on the site; just those that appear in the navigation menu inside list items. We can therefore create a new selector in the style sheet that only changes links found in the list items of the main menu ID, in much the same way as we did in the last chapter:

#mainmenu li a {

}

(Remember that "a" relates to links).

This only modifies links found in the list items inside the main menu ID, and will not interfere with any links outside of it.

Now, the underline is set by the "text-decoration" property of the links, so we need to remove the text decoration.

text-decoration: none;

Here is how the new menu looks:

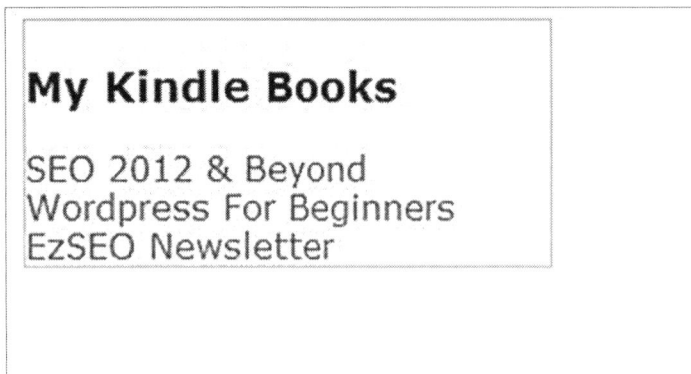

My Kindle Books

SEO 2012 & Beyond
Wordpress For Beginners
EzSEO Newsletter

(19.1.html and 19.1.css)

This is all very well, but there's no great visual indicator for the visitor to know which item in the menu the mouse is hovering over. Load the HTML file in your browser and try it. Move your mouse over the links in the menu. The cursor changes to a pointing hand, but it's not very inspiring, is it? So let's change it to something that feels more interactive.

We will begin by putting a box around each list item and giving it a color. We can do this by creating a new selector for list items in "main menu", and by adding a border:

```
#mainmenu li {
        border: 1px solid Blue;
        background: #A8A9FF;
}
```

This gives each menu item both a border and background color.

Here is how the menu looks now:

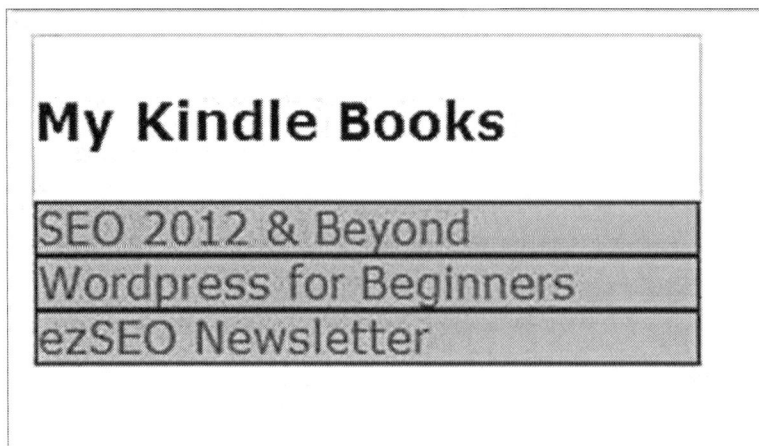

My Kindle Books

SEO 2012 & Beyond
Wordpress for Beginners
ezSEO Newsletter

(19.2.html and 19.2.css)

Since we have now put a border around each of the menu items, we no longer need the border around the #mainmenu ID. So let us remove this line from that section of the style sheet:

border: thin dashed Silver;

While we are at it, let's change the menu item text to white, so that it contrasts nicely with the background. To do that, we simply add the following line to the "#mainmenu li "a" section of our style sheet:

color: White;

Here is how our modified menu looks:

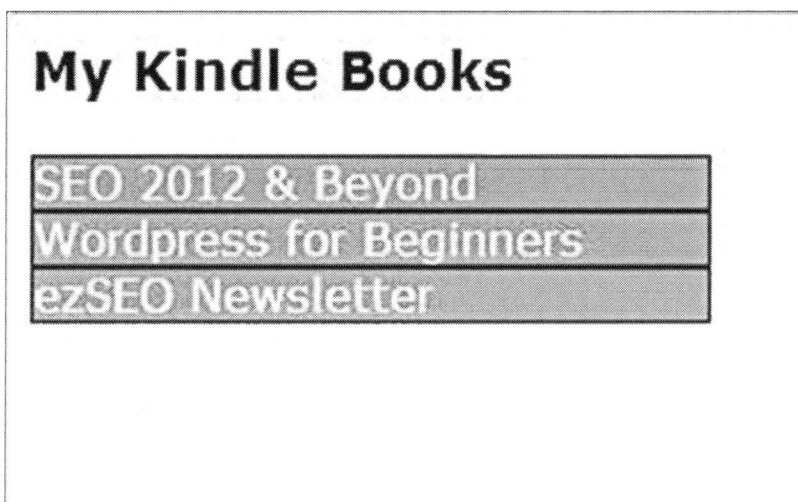

(19.3.html and 19.3.css)

We still don't have a rollover effect to show the visitor which menu item the mouse is over, so let's do that now.

Do you remember earlier when we were covering pseudo classes? The HTML element "a" had several pseudo classes that refer to the state of the link.

What we want to do here is to add a visual effect when the mouse is hovered over a link. Therefore we need the **a:hover** pseudo class, but only for links in list items, and only when it occurs in the main menu.

Here is the selector we need to define in our style sheets:

#mainmenu li a:hover {

}

Let's now change the background color white, and the link text color to the original background color.

```
#mainmenu li a:hover {
    color:#A8A9FF;
    background-color: white;
}
```

Here is how our menu looks now on mouseover:

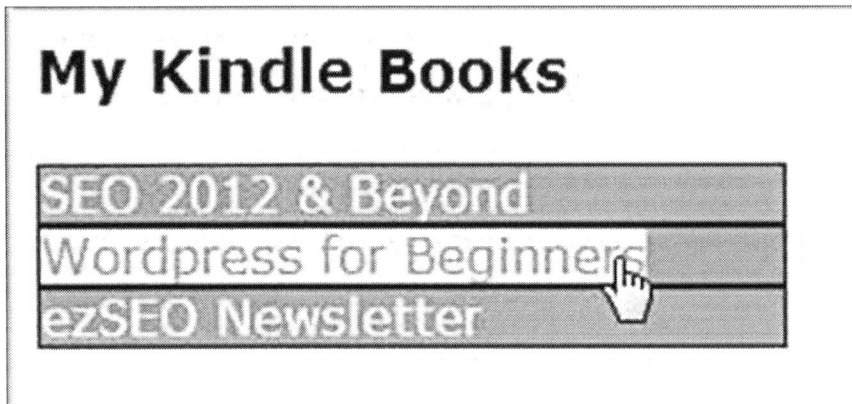

(19.4.html and 19.4.css)

As you can see, I've moved my mouse over the second link in the menu to illustrate the desired effect.

Moving the mouse over each menu item does do what we want, but wouldn't it be nicer if the whole of that line turned white instead of just the text area? Well, with CSS we can fix that too. All we need to do is to tell the web browser to treat the whole of the link in the list item as a single block.

To do that, add the following line to the "#mainmenu li "a" selector:

display: block;

Here is how our finished menu behaves on mouseover:

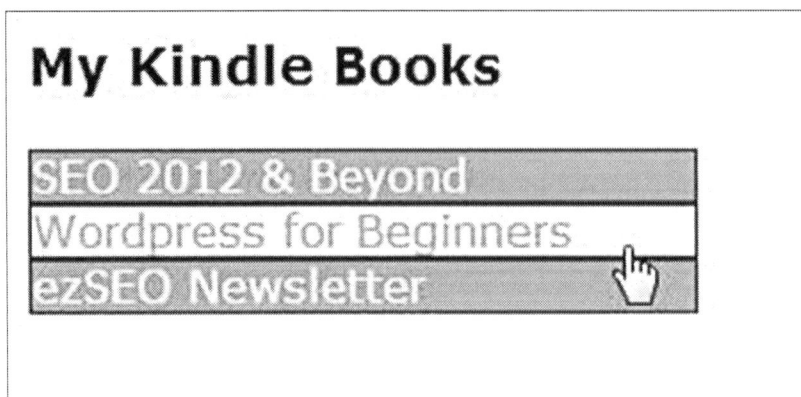

(19.5.html and 19.5.css)

See how the whole row turns white now? That's much neater.

You can experiment with borders, colors, and any other properties available to you in CSS to make your menus fit your wcb page template. In other words, what type of menu you create is limited only by your imagination,

In the next chapter, we will look at how you can use lists to create horizontal menus. These types of menus are ideal for using across the top of your pages, or indeed at the bottom, depending on your objectives.

20. Creating Horizontal Menus Using Lists

Here is the vertical menu we created in the last chapter:

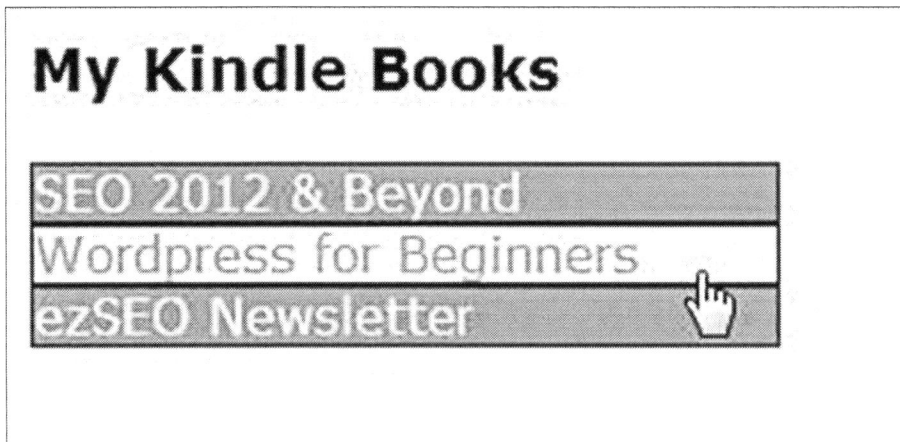

(19.5.html and 19.5.css)

Let's now look at how to create a horizontal menu.

We will start off with the same HTML file as the original vertical menu, and just create a new style sheet. To save a bit of time, we can take the old vertical style sheet, and delete all of the properties from the selectors. This will give us a blank canvas to work from:

Here is how my emptied style sheet looks:

```
#mainmenu {
}
#mainmenu ul {
}
#mainmenu li {
}
#mainmenu li a {
}
#mainmenu li a:hover {
}
```

Let's begin by defining the mainmenu ID again. We will keep the same font family and padding as before:

        font-family: Verdana, Geneva, Arial, Helvetica, sans-serif;

        padding: 10px;

One item we have removed is the width property. We only included that in the original menu to restrict it to a narrow column on our web page. The horizontal menu, on the other hand, needs to stretch across the page.

For the "#mainmenu ul", we use the same properties:

list-style: none;
margin: 0px;

Now, we need to do something different in the "#mainmenu li" selector. Here, we have to tell the web browser not to move each list item onto a new line. We can achieve this by using the display property, and set it to "inline".

#mainmenu li {
        display: inline;
}

Here is how our horizontal menu looks so far:

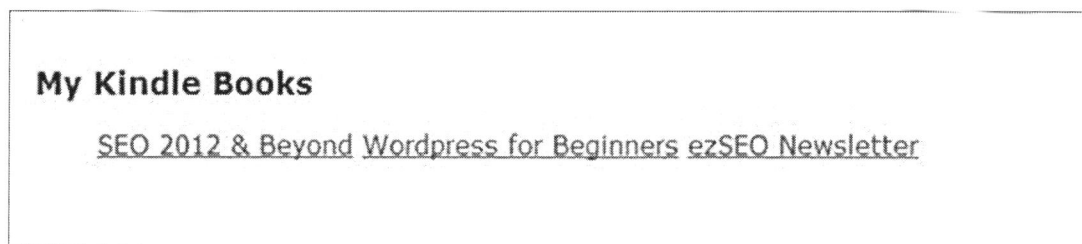

My Kindle Books

SEO 2012 & Beyond Wordpress for Beginners ezSEO Newsletter

(20.1.html and 20.1.css)

We have a horizontal menu, but we now need to add the formatting that gives us the mouseover effects. I'll also add in some properties to turn the links into "buttons", as we did with the vertical menu.

In the "#mainmenu li a" selector, we can add our borders, colors, and also remove the underline:

text-decoration: none;
border: 1px solid Blue;
background: #A8A9FF;
padding: 5px;
margin: 2px;
color: white;

Here is how our horizontal menu looks now:

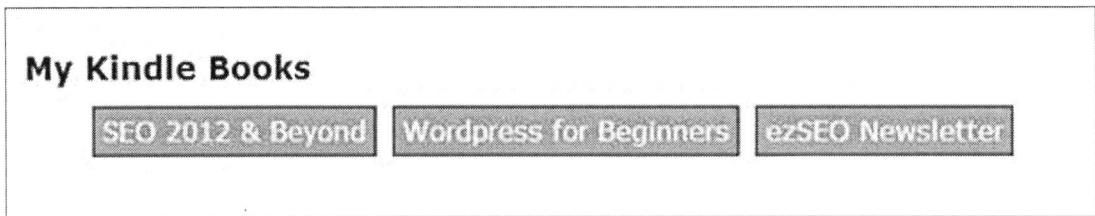

(20.2.html and 20.2.css)

We are almost there now. The only thing left to do is add the mouseover effect that will change the background and font colors. We do this by adding the following code to the "#mainmenu li a:hover " selector:

```
color:#A8A9FF;
background-color: white;
```

And here is our completed horizontal menu:

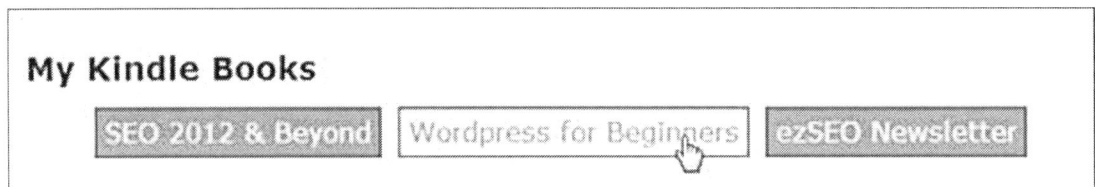

(20.3.html and 20.3.css)

This last example shows how to make the links look more like buttons by the clever use of the border color properties:

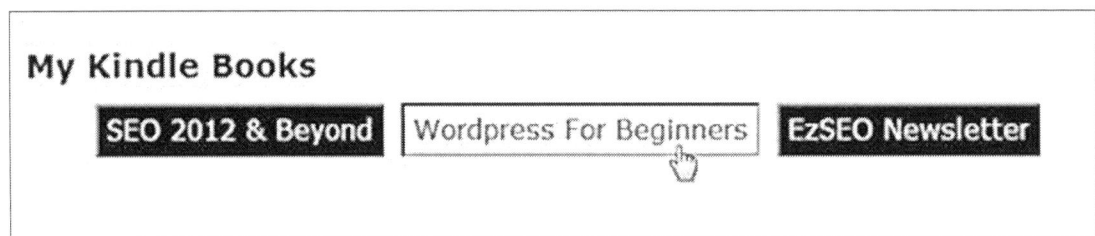

(20.4.html and 20.4.css)

Feel free to examine the CSS code, and use it as is, or modify it for use on your own templates.

21. Fixing the Position of a Box

Imagine that you have a subscription form in the right sidebar of your site. As a visitor scrolls down the page reading your content, the subscription form scrolls up and off the page (out of view).

What if you could make the subscription form so that it was always visible? Well, you can do that with CSS too.

We have already seen absolute positioning. This time we need to make the position of the box **fixed**.

Let's look at an example:

As the visitor scrolls down, reading the content, the position of the subscription box remains in the same position, that is, it scrolls down with the reader, meaning it's always visible.

Here you can see the subscription box near the footer:

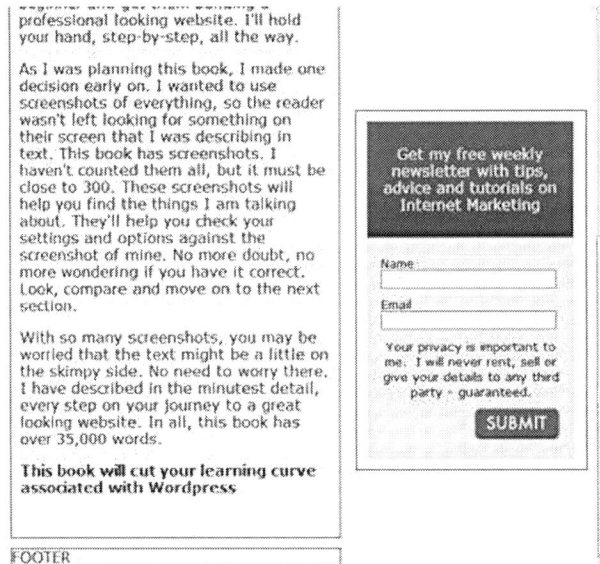

To achieve this effect, simply set the position of the menu in your style sheet:

Position: fixed;

(21.1.html and 21.1.css)

NOTE: Wait for this to load as the subscription form is a JavaScript.

This CSS code is almost identical to the code we saw earlier in chapter 17. The only difference is the position has been changed to "fixed" for the right menu:

```
] #rightmenu {border: thin solid black;
 Position : fixed;
 top: 110px;
 right: 10px;
 width: 25%;
 padding: 10px;
-}
] #leftmenu {border: thin solid black;
 position:absolute;
 top: 110px;
 left: 10px;
 width: 25%;
 padding: 10px;
-}
```

Load the html file in your browser and see how this works.

22. Playing with Background Images

Using background images in your templates is very easy. You can add a background image to the entire web page, or just a box on the page.

To add a background image to the entire page, add a body { } section to your CSS file. You then need to add a background-image selector, with the URL of the image to be used. In my example, the image is saved in the same folder as the web page that is using it.

Body { background-image:url ('smilie.jpg');
}

Here is the effect:

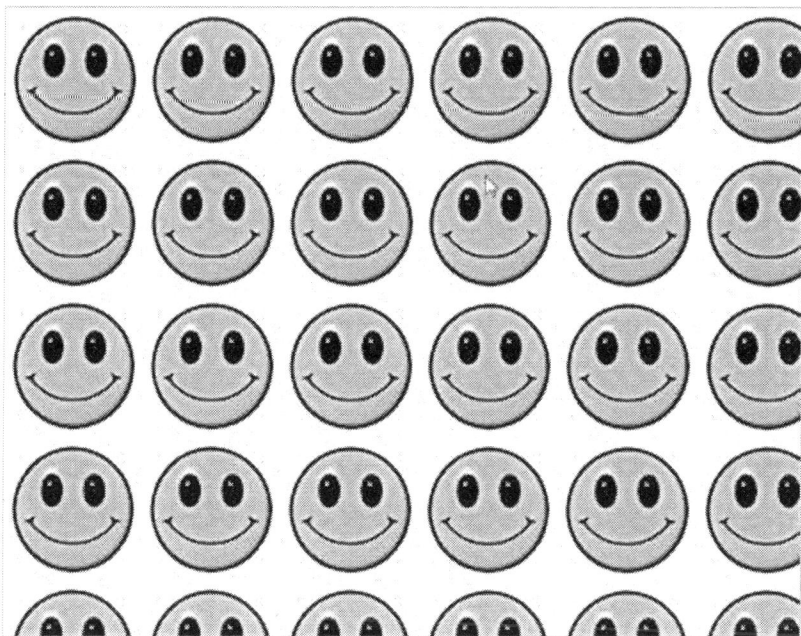

(21.1.html and 21.1.css)

Now, by default, the image is tiled (repeated) over the whole page. We can change this by using the "background-repeat" style. There are various options.

Here are some web pages using the different choices:

background-repeat: no-repeat; (image is not repeated)

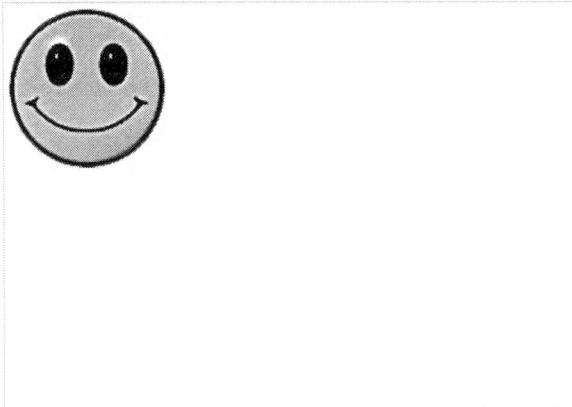

background-repeat: repeat-x; (image is only repeated horizontally)

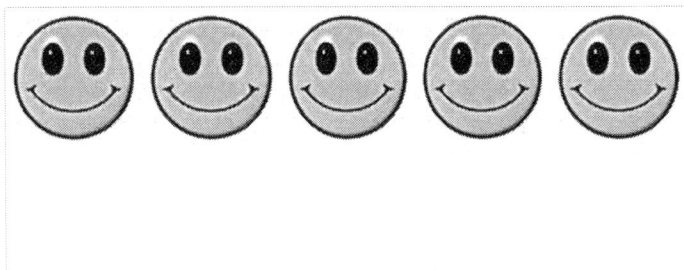

background-repeat: repeat-y; (mage is only repeated vertically)

Interesting effects!

You can have the image "fixed" in the background, so they don't scroll with the text by adding this property:

background-attachment: fixed;

Or, you can have the image scroll with the text by adding this property:

background-attachment: scroll;

I'll leave those for you to explore on your own.

In the illustrations above, we have shown how the whole body section of the web page can be affected. We can also limit these effects to boxes on the screen, by creating a DIV section on the page, and then applying the CSS code to a class or ID that will control the DIV.

Have a look at this example:

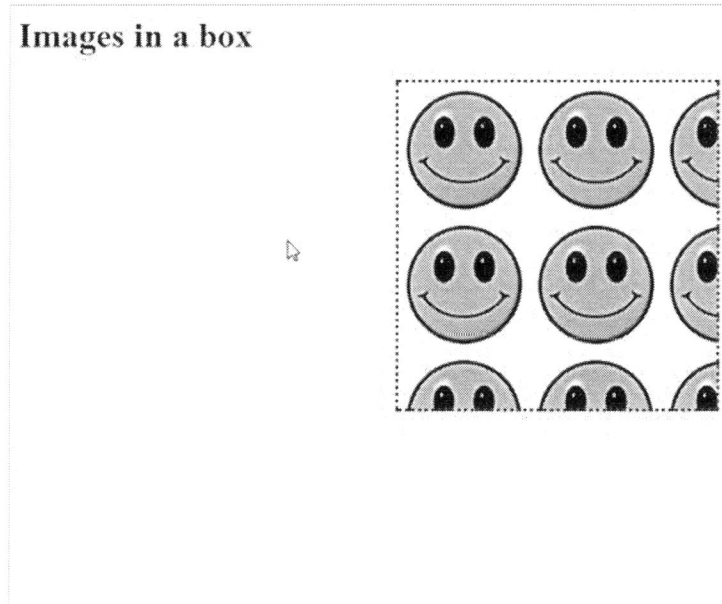

(22.2.html and 22.2.css)

Take a look at the code behind this effect. You will see that we have a lot of control over image backgrounds, so have some fun!

23. Using an Image As the Bullet of a List

When you are designing a web template, you might want to customize the bullet points on the lists used on your pages. A great way of doing this is to use a custom image for the bullet. In this example, I am going to change the bullets of a list from the default circle, to a smiley face 

We need to use an "unordered" list as we want bullets. (23.1.html and 23.1.css)

We need to create a selector for the "ul" html element. We then want to modify the list-style-image property to point to our smilie graphic:

```
ul {    list-style-image: url(smilie2.gif);
}
```

Here is the page:

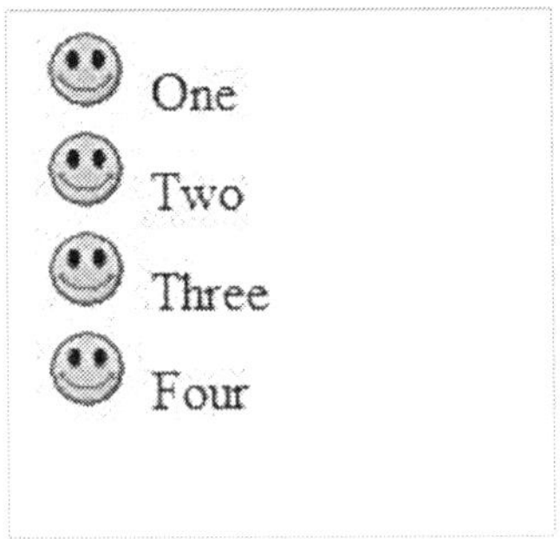

(23.2.html and 23.2.css)

24. Congratulations!

If you have made it this far, you are no longer a beginner at CSS. Of course, there is plenty more you can learn about Cascading Style Sheets, but you have enough knowledge now to start exploring the CSS code powering other websites, and maybe even grab some ideas of your own from them.

Have you ever been to a webpage and wondered how they achieved a certain effect? Ever wanted to change the look of your own website but wasn't sure how? Then this section is for you. We are going to look at some real pages and uncover the CSS behind them. We will find some interesting effects, and see just how we can replicate those same effects on our own website.

Google Chrome Developer Tools

Google Chrome is a free web browser, but it offers more than just a window into the web. It also has some Chrome Developer Tools built in that are invaluable for helping you to work out how various effects are achieved on a webpage. You can use Chrome to help change the look of your own website, or investigate how a site accomplishes a particularly interesting effect.

In this section of the CSS for Beginners course, I want to show you how to use the built-in features of Google Chrome. This will help you become confident fiddling with CSS code; code that may help you to make some interesting changes on your own website. If you haven't already, download and install Chrome:

https://www.google.com/intl/en/chrome/browser/

Once Google Chrome is installed, press the F12 key (or CTRL+SHIFT+I), to open the Developer Tools we will be using. Your screen will become split horizontally, and the tools are opened at the bottom of the chrome window:

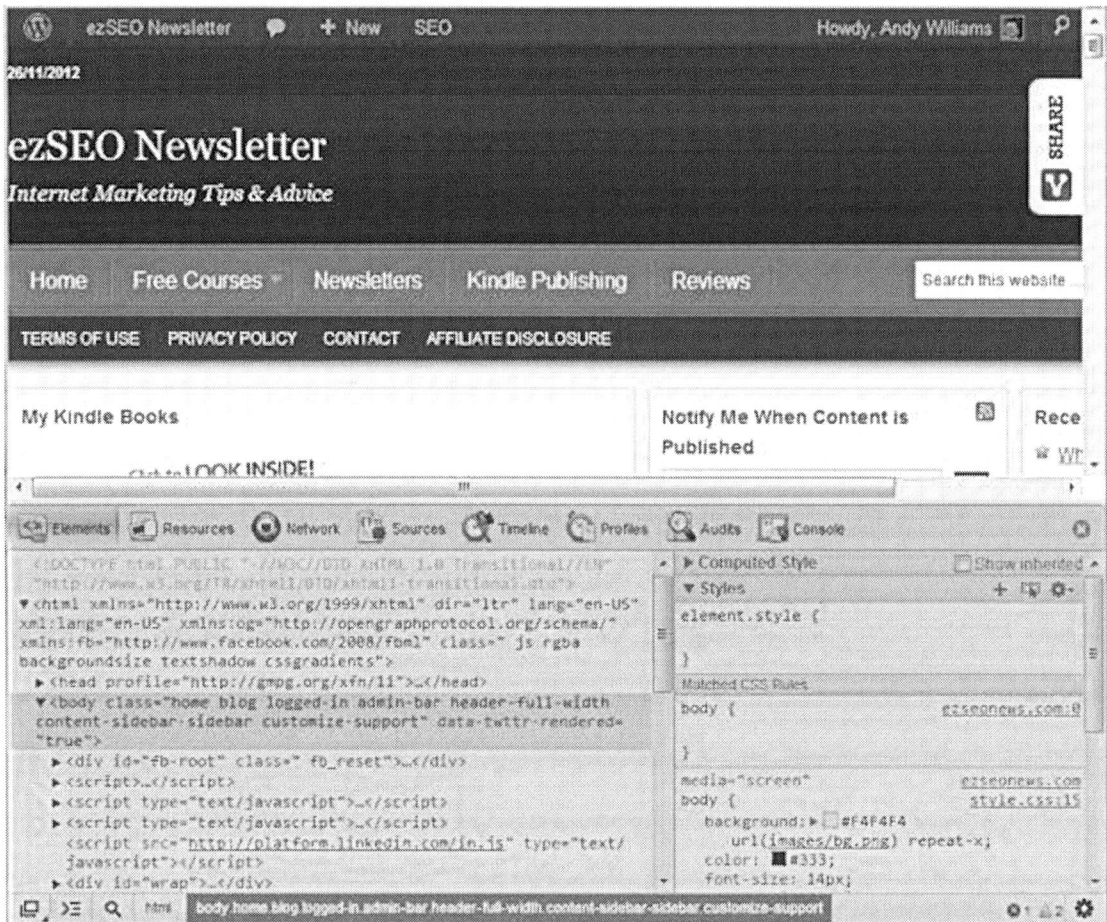

So the lower half of the screen shows the tools, and the upper part shows a preview of the web page you are looking at.

Google Chrome Developer Tools - Video Tutorials

I have recorded some videos that you can access here:

http://ezseonews.com/css

These videos take you through a variety of tasks that you can perform using the Chrome Dev Tools. These tools will help you better understand the CSS behind any website. They really are incredibly powerful for web developers, but I'll just concentrate here on what you need for exploring HTML and CSS.

Summary

This Guide to CSS is intended to be a hands-on tutorial, where you create the pages for yourself, and experiment. This is by far the best way to learn CSS.

I hope you have enjoyed the course, and that you are excited about getting to learn more about the power of using CSS on your own website(s). It is a great toolset to have in your locker, and not only is it fun to use, but it will also save you having to pay others to carry out CSS tasks for you.

There is so much we could not cover in this tutorial, but at least now you have enough knowledge to go out and create your own CSS templates, and confidently seek help online whenever you need it.

Appendix

Download ALL source code shown in this book from:

http://ezseonews.com/css

On that page you will find a download link to all of the source code from this book. The first video on that page shows you how to use this source code.

Please Review This Book on Amazon:

If you enjoyed this book, please leave a review on Amazon.

Search Amazon for **B00AFV44NS**

Thanks in advance!

My other Kindle books

Wordpress for Beginners

Do you want to build a website but scared it's too difficult?

Building a website was once the domain of computer geeks. Not anymore. WordPress makes it possible for anyone to create and run a professional looking website

While WordPress is an amazing tool, the truth is it does have a steep learning curve, even if you have built websites before using different tools. Therefore, the goal of this book is to take anyone, even a complete beginner, and get them building a professional looking website. I'll hold your hand, step-by-step, all the way.

As I was planning this book, I made one decision early on. I wanted to use screenshots of everything so that the reader wasn't left looking for something on their screen that I was describing in text. This book has plenty of screenshots. I haven't counted them all, but it must be close to 300. These images will help you find the things I am talking about. They'll help you check your settings and options against the screenshot of mine. You look, compare, and move on to the next section.

With so many screenshots, you may be concerned that the text might be a little on the skimpy side. No need to worry there. I have described every step of your journey in great detail. In all, this publication has over 35,000 words.

This book will surely cut your learning curve associated with WordPress.

Every chapter of the book ends with a "Tasks to Complete" section. By completing these tasks, you'll not only become proficient at using WordPress, but you'll become confident & enjoy using it too.

Search Amazon for **B009ZVO3H6**

Wordpress SEO

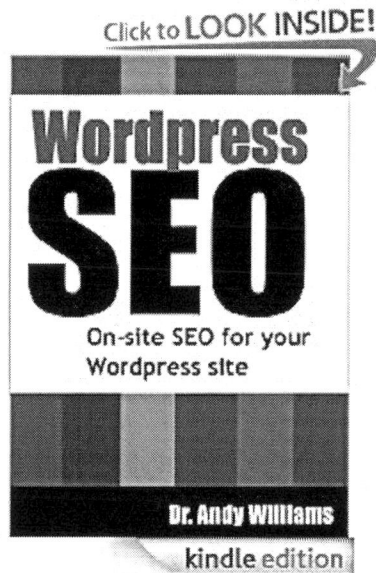

On-Page SEO for your Wordpress Site

Most websites (including blogs) share certain features that can be controlled and used to help (or hinder, especially with Google Panda & Penguin on the loose) with the on-site SEO. These features include things like the page title, headlines, body text, ALT tags and so on. In this respect, most sites can be treated in a similar manner when we consider on-site SEO.

However, different platforms have their own quirks, and WordPress is no exception. Out-of-the-box WordPress doesn't do itself any SEO favours, and can in fact cause you ranking problems, especially with the potentially huge amount of duplicate content it creates. Other problems include static, site-wide sidebars and footers, automatically generated meta tags, page load speeds, SEO issues with Wordpress themes, poorly constructed navigation, badly designed homepages, potential spam from visitors, etc. The list goes on.

This book shows you how to set up an SEO-friendly Wordpress website, highlighting the problems, and working through them with step-by-step instructions on how to fix them.

By the end of this book, your WordPress site should be well optimized, without being 'over-optimized' (which is itself a contributing factor in Google penalties).

Search Amazon for: **B00ECF70HU**

SEO 2013 & Beyond

Search Engine Optimization will never be the Same Again!

On February 11th, 2011, Google dropped a bombshell on the SEO community when they released the Panda update. Panda was designed to remove low quality content from the search engine results pages. The surprise to many webmasters were some of the big name casualties that got taken out by the update.

On 24th April 2012, Google went in for the kill when they released the Penguin update. Few SEOs that had been in the business for any length of time could believe the carnage that this update caused. If Google's Panda was a 1 on the Richter scale of updates, Penguin was surely a 10. It completely changed the way we needed to think about SEO.

On September 28th 2012, Google released a new algorithm update targeting exact match domains (EMDs). I have updated this book to let you know the consequences of owning EMDs, and added my own advice on choosing domain names. While I have never been a huge fan of exact match domains anyway, many other SEO books and courses teach you to use them. I'll tell you why I think those other courses and books are wrong. The EMD update was sandwiched in between another Panda update (on the 27th September) and another Penguin update (5th October).

Whereas Panda seems to penalize low quality content, Penguin is more concerned about overly aggressive SEO tactics. The stuff that SEOs had been doing for years, not only didn't work anymore, but could now actually cause your site to be penalized and drop out of the rankings. That's right, just about everything you have been taught about Search Engine Optimization in the last 10 years can be thrown out the Window. Google have moved the goal posts.

I have been working in SEO for around 10 years at the time of writing, and have always tried to stay within the guidelines laid down by Google. This has not always been easy because to compete with other sites, it often meant using techniques that Google frowned upon. Now, if you use those techniques, Google is likely to catch up with you and demote your rankings. In this book, I want to share with you the new SEO. The SEO for 2013 and Beyond.

Search Amazon for **B0099RKXE8**

An SEO Checklist

A step-by-step plan for fixing SEO problems with your web site

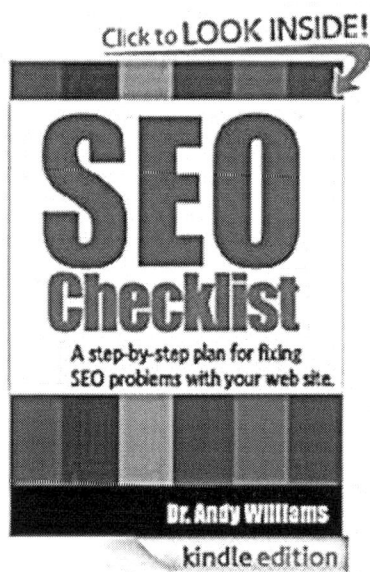

A step-by-step plan for fixing SEO problems with your web site

Pre-Panda and pre-Penguin, Google tolerated certain activities. Post-Panda and post-Penguin, they don't. As a result, they are now enforcing their Webmaster Guidelines which is something that SEOs never really believed Google would do! Essentially, Google have become far less tolerant of activities that they see as rank manipulation.

As webmasters, we have been given a choice. Stick to Google's rules, or lose out on free traffic from the world's biggest search engine.

Those that had abused the rules in the past got a massive shock. Their website(s), which may have been at the top of Google for several years, dropped like a stone. Rankings gone, literally overnight!

To have any chance of recovery, you MUST clean up that site. However, for most people, trying to untangle the SEO mess that was built up over several years is not always easy. Where do you start?

That's why this book was written. It provides a step-by-step plan to fix a broken site. This book contains detailed checklists plus an explanation of why those things are so important.

The checklists in this book are based on the SEO that I use on a daily basis. It's the SEO I teach my students, and it's the SEO that I know works. For those that embrace the recent changes, SEO has actually become easier as we no longer have to battle against other sites whose SEO was done 24/7 by an automated tool or an army of cheap labor. Those sites have largely been removed, and that has leveled the playing field.

If you have a site that lost its rankings, this book gives you a step-by-step plan and checklist to fix problems that are common causes of ranking penalties.

Search Amazon for **B00BXFAULK**

Kindle Publishing

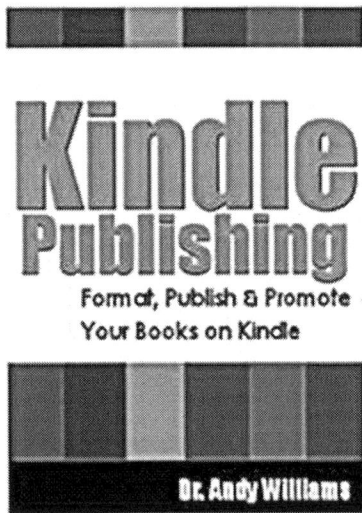

Format, Publish & Promote your books on Kindle

Why Publish on Amazon Kindle?

Kindle publishing has captured the imagination of aspiring writers. Now, more than at any other time in our history, an opportunity is knocking. Getting your books published no longer means sending out hundreds of letters to publishers and agents. It no longer means getting hundreds of rejection letters back. Today, you can write and publish your own books on Amazon Kindle without an agent or publisher.

Is it Really Possible to Make a Good Income as an Indie Author?

The fact that you are reading this book description tells me you are interested in publishing your own material on Kindle. You may have been lured here by promises of quick riches. Well, I have good news and bad. The bad news is that publishing and profiting from Kindle takes work and dedication. Don't just expect to throw up sub-par material and make a killing in sales. You need to produce good stuff to be successful at this. The good news is that you can make a very decent living from writing and publishing on Kindle.

My own success with Kindle Publishing

As I explain at the beginning of this book, I published my first Kindle book in August 2012, yet by December 2012, just 5 months later, I was making what many people consider being a full time income. As part of my own learning experience, I setup a Facebook page in July 2012 to share my Kindle publishing journey (there is a link to the Facebook page inside this book). On that Facebook page, I shared the details of what I did, and problems I needed to overcome. I also shared my growing income reports, and most of all, I offered help to those who asked for it. What I found was a huge and growing audience for this type of education, and ultimately, that's why I wrote this book.

What's in this Book?

This book covers what I have learned on my journey and what has worked for me. I have included sections to answer the questions I myself asked, as well as those questions people asked me. This book is a complete reference manual for successfully formatting, publishing & promoting your books on Amazon Kindle. There is even a section for non-US publishers because there is stuff there you specifically need to know. I see enormous potential in Kindle Publishing, and in 2013 I intend to grow this side of my own business. Kindle publishing has been liberating for me and I am sure it will be for you too.

Search Amazon for **B00BEIX34C**

Migrating to Windows 8

For computer users without a touch screen, coming from XP, Vista or Windows 7

Review: "What Microsoft should buy and give away now to drive sales"

New PCs are coming pre-installed with Windows 8, Microsoft's new incarnation of the popular operating system. The problem is, the PCs it is installed on are not usually equipped with the piece of hardware that Windows 8 revolves around - a touch screen.

Windows 8 is probably the least user-friendly version of the operating system ever released. It's almost like two different operating systems merged together. From the lack of a start menu, to features that only really make sense on a tablet or phone, Windows 8 has a lot of veteran Windows users scratching their heads. If you are one of them, then this book is for you.

After a quick tour of the new user interface, the book digs deeper into the features of Windows 8, showing you what everything does, and more importantly, how to do the things you used to do on older versions of Windows. The comprehensive "How to" section answers a lot of the questions new users have, and there's also a complete keyboard shortcut list for reference.

If you are migrating to Windows 8 from XP, Vista or Windows 7, then this book may just let you keep your hair as you learn how to get the most out of your computer. Who knows, you may even get to like Windows 8.

Search Amazon for **B00CJ8AD9E**

More information from Dr. Andy Williams

If you would like more information, tips, tutorials or advice, there are two resources you might like to consider.

The first is my free weekly newsletter over at ezSEONews.com offering tips, tutorials and advice to online marketers and webmasters. Just sign up and my newsletter, plus SEO articles, will be delivered to your inbox. I cannot always promise a weekly schedule, but I do try ;)

I also run a course over at CreatingFatContent.com, where I build real websites in front of members in "real-time" using my system of SEO.

Printed in Great Britain
by Amazon